COMPASSIONATE CAPITALISM

A Journey to the Soul of Business

Blaine Bartlett
and
David Meltzer

Published by Best Seller Publishing®, Pasadena, CA
Best Seller Publishing® is a registered trademark
Printed in the United States of America.
ISBN-13: 978-1535241083
ISBN-10: 153524108X

This publication is designed to provide accurate and authoritative information with regard to the subject matter covered. It is sold with the understanding that the publisher is not engaged in rendering legal, accounting, or other professional advice. If legal advice or other expert assistance is required, the services of a competent professional should be sought. The opinions expressed by the authors in this book are not endorsed by Best Seller Publishing® and are the sole responsibility of the author rendering the opinion.

Most Best Seller Publishing® titles are available at special quantity discounts for bulk purchases for sales promotions, premiums, fundraising, and educational use. Special versions or book excerpts can also be created to fit specific needs.

For more information, please write:
Best Seller Publishing®
1346 Walnut Street, #205
Pasadena, CA 91106
or call 1(626) 765 9750
Toll Free: 1(844) 850-3500
Visit us online at: www.BestSellerPublishing.org

Endorsements

I LOVE THIS BOOK!!!! Thank you so much for writing the truth and saying what every living breathing person knows MUST be said. You are my hero. Thank-you so much. I hope it goes right to the top of every single chart. Really! Bravissimo!

~ Lynne Twist, NY Times best-selling author of *The Soul of Money*, Founder of The Soul of Money Institute and co-founder of Pachamama Alliance

Bartlett and Meltzer offer us a compelling case for a new way of thinking rooted in the truth that all things are connected. *Compassionate Capitalism* provides great lessons from early adopters on this path toward truly sustainable growth and encourages those still waiting to jump in.

~ Rick Miller, former President AT&T Global and Chief at BeingChief.com

This book is about the crucial intersections of business, life, and the true essence of the human spirit. What Bartlett and Meltzer present represents business intentionally and compassionately making the future our business. It is must reading for any leader – in and out of business!

~ Andrew Black, founder/CEO of BrandProject, co-founder Virgin Mobile Canada with Sir Richard Branson, and former President Americas at LEGO

Business leaders now have a guidebook that can transform the way business is conducted on the planet for the benefit of all. I encourage you to read this and circulate a copy to anyone with whom you do business…it's that good!

~ Dr. Ivan Misner, Founder of BNI
and NY Times bestselling author

Compassionate Capitalism is an important contribution to our growing understanding of what it will take make business a force for healing and uplifting the human condition in the future. Too many businesses have lost sight of the fact that the flourishing of lives is the ultimate purpose; this book shows how we can help make that a reality.

~ Raj Sisodia, professor, Babson College;
co-founder Conscious Capitalism Inc.

Compassionate Capitalism redefines what it means to create value. A wonderfully optimistic guide to moving from surviving to thriving through compassionate leadership of business, employees, customers, and the planet. A must read for those creating the future of business!

~ Bruce MacGregor, CCO and Managing Partner for Asia at IDEO

This book is not only timely; it must become required reading for anyone leading or aspiring to lead a business. The significant issues we face today can be solved by business and this book provides a prescription for doing so. Get it and apply it.

~ Jack Canfield, Coauthor of *The Success Principles*, *Heart at Work*, and the *Chicken Soup for the Soul* series

Bartlett and Meltzer raise bold and important questions about today's business climate in their intriguing new book, *Compassionate Capitalism*. Founded on the four pillars of gratitude, empathy, accountability and effective communication, this book offers real solutions for transforming organizations into more purposeful entities for the future."

~ Stephen M. R. Covey, The NY Times bestselling author of
The Speed of Trust and coauthor of *Smart Trust*

In *Compassionate Capitalism*, Bartlett and Meltzer eloquently amplify the Quadruple Bottom Line concept (people, planet, profit and purpose) by redefining business as a spiritual discipline lead by "merchant priests" and by outlining an action plan for negotiating the essential transition from an economy of scarcity to an economy of abundance. In essence, they have created a business plan for a sustainable future. Given the ubiquitous toxic consequences of Industrial Capitalism, the fate of humanity literally hinges upon our ability to heed their sage advice.

~ Rinaldo S. Brutoco, Founder and President
World Business Academy

Profit matters, but our world matters more. *Compassionate Capitalism* powerfully illustrates how compassion is a vital key to sustainable economic growth. I love this book! It's a must read book for business leaders everywhere.

~ Cynthia Kersey, Best-selling author of *Unstoppable* and
Founder and CEO Unstoppable Foundation

This books shifts the paradigm of international business. The world will never be the same!

~ Kishore Lulla, Chairman and CEO Eros International Group

Touchdown! Bartlett to Meltzer!

~ Warren Moon, President, Sports 1 Marketing,
NFL Hall of Fame Quarterback,
and Founder of the Crescent Moon Foundation

Table of Contents

Preface

The Unacknowledged Purpose of Business

Today, the default focus for almost every business in operation is the creation of profits. This focus is so pervasive in the paradigm that defines business, the purpose of business being to make a profit has essentially become gospel (a tip of the hat to economist Milton Friedman). Ever-increasing quarterly returns are the metric by which success is assessed; return on investment (ROI) is a sacred litmus test for any activity; company "value" (as measured by both market-cap and price-to-earning (P/E) ratios) has become, for many, practically the only way investment quality and the quality of the business is measured. This has created a destructive reinforcing cycle that compromises—even negates—what I believe is the true purpose of business: *to uplift the experience of existing*. It is not to make owners wealthy. It is not to produce ever-cheaper goods and services. It is not to keep an avaricious and toxic economic model afloat. And it is certainly not (with no apology to Milton Friedman) to make massive profits.

Business is the most pervasive and influential force on the planet today. Its activities transcend national and international borders. Its enterprises are not unduly constrained by financial, political, cultural, ethnic, or religious concerns. The net of this is that business, as a prevalent and important force, has a moral responsibility to guide, enhance, value, and nourish the existence of all that it encounters. In the world today, the absolute opposite of this often occurs. Business today seldom assesses the efficacy of its activities through the lens of anything but profit.

Because business touches literally everything that humans are involved with, its activity rises to a level approaching that of a spiritual undertaking. I mean this not in any woo-woo or religious sense, however. Rather, I mean this in the pragmatic sense that everything on this planet—organic/inorganic, sentient/nonsentient—is connected in subtle but profound ways that can only be fully appreciated through a lens of spiritual compassion.

Either harmful acts or ennobling acts undertaken by business affects everything and everyone in some fashion. Nothing we encounter is separate and isolated from the whole. We live in and on a closed system that is fully and symbiotically integrated. Consequently, we and everything else on this planet we call home are dependent on the viability of each constituent part.

From our perspective, business is nothing less than a spiritual discipline, therefore it requires the same integrity, commitment, intentionality, courage, and compassion. Spiritual disciplines honor life, in all its forms, as having innate and intrinsic value simply because it exists. It's the honoring of this value—the ennobling of this value—that is called forth when we approach business as a spiritual undertaking. It is the compassionate thing to do.

~ Blaine Bartlett

Introduction

We are but a network of relationships and these alone matter to us.
~ Antoine de Saint-Exupéry, adapted

The authors of this book have collectively spent an aggregate of more than 80 years witnessing the consequences of apathy, emotional disengagement, autocratic leaders, and mindless pursuit of short-term goals that have no intrinsic meaning outside of enhancing quarterly results. Those consequences are toxic to:

- The environment.
- Employees.
- Families.
- Society.
- The long-term vibrancy and health of humankind.
- And ultimately to all life on the planet.

What else can we say? Most organizations are toxic to both the human spirit and the human condition. The results produced by capitalism, socialism, communism, or any other *ism* that we care to name, are also reported and expressed through their organizations. They focus on short-term goals, to produce results with scant concern for interests other than the shareholders. They value profits and ideology above all else. And the view that employees, natural resources, and time are disposable components, intended for use in the relentless drive to ever-increasing success, contribute greatly to this malaise.

Yes, much good has been produced by many organizations; but at the same time, many leave behind the debris of corporate greed that can take decades or centuries to undo. This isn't cynicism. It's fact. Read the newspaper. But don't get us wrong: we love business. Organizations fascinate us professionally. We are all social beings, and who we are and how we live and work is, in large part, defined by how we organize. And the way that most companies have evolved their ways of conducting business has gone seriously off the rails.

What went wrong? That's part of the focus of this book. We will also be suggesting a few ideas to set things back on track. We propose nothing short of a revolution in our most fundamental attitudes toward capitalism as an economic model, our understanding of the purpose of the businesses it has spawned, and the role and definition of what it means to be a leader.

Any organization is complex. Even something as simple as an individual, or a couple, can potentially exhibit the complex organizational dynamics of large global enterprises. There are hierarchies that inform who does what. There are values and rules that guide both decision making and behavior. Goals are determined within the context of the purpose for being together. Results are evaluated and either rewarded or punished. And communication problems never seem to end.

There's an old organizational development joke that says, "We designed the perfect organization, then screwed it up by putting people in it." The human spirit doesn't take kindly to captivity. People are infinitely complex. Each of us potentially represents the proto-organization. When all our organizational systems work in coherence and harmony is when the various parts that make you *you* coordinate well. The organization that I call *me* is healthy, vibrant, at ease, creative, growing, and generally set up to work well and thrive. This same phenomenon is true of both a simple at-home business and complex global organizations.

This brings us to the question of leadership and how organizations are led. What is the responsibility of leadership in today's world? Who is the leader ultimately responsible for how any organization produces results? Here's a thought: There are no leadership positions to be had in an organization. There are, however, positions of ever-increasing authority. These are not the same thing.

Blaine has studied leadership in individuals and organizations for almost 40 years, and it has led him to the conclusion that leadership is embodied in every one of us; it is exerted at every level by every person in an organization, regardless of position or title. The short version about who's the leader responsible is this: *everyone's a leader.*

Now let's examine this assertion a bit. When all is said and done, leaders cause movement. Of course, they do it in a variety of ways. Personalities vary. Situations call for different approaches. Unfortunately, yelling is a favorite of many. Command and control is often valued. Empowerment is offered, threats are made, and rewards are offered. To paraphrase: Some of these ways work some of the time, but none of them work all the time. And again, these are all simply ways in which movement is produced. The logical implication is that they are not necessarily the ways that leaders can count on to produce the movement necessary to effect the desired results. Movement and results are different activities.

We define *leadership* as the activity of causing coordinated movement that produces actions necessary to achieve the desired results. Based on this definition, everyone in any organization is a leader, simply because their presence causes movement of some sort. Therefore, when we speak of leadership development, we are actually addressing the issue of leadership effectiveness. Does the resulting movement enable coordination with others in a manner that causes the necessary actions required to get the desired results *without* costly unintended consequences (in terms of time, money, and relationship angst) that need to be addressed? Coordinated movement is the measure of effectiveness. In its highest form, it calls for compassionate (and some would say spiritual) engagement with other stakeholders.

Referring to leadership as a position or role that is to be occupied or taken on implies that one is or isn't a leader until he or she occupies a certain position or title. This is why most leadership development activities are reserved for certain people at a certain level in the organization. It is also why focusing on specific roles for leadership development have a limited ROI, compared to what would be possible if a broader approach were taken. It tends to minimize the role coordinated movement plays in defining leadership and its effectiveness.

Linking leadership to roles and positions does harm in four ways; it:

- Separates the activity of leadership from the holistic and legitimate *being-ness* of an individual.
- Divorces individuals from rightfully taking responsibility for the results they find being created around them.
- Excludes the development of leadership effectiveness as a universal and legitimate aspiration for all in an organization and in life.
- Limits conversation about and explorations of leadership to only the "deserving," and disempowers entire populations.

We all cause continuous movement in our lives, therefore we are all leaders and accordingly responsible for the results in our organization. Most of us are not likely to be as effective with our leadership activities as we could be, or would like to be.

Delinking leadership from roles and positions creates the possibility of tapping enormous potential in almost every organization. If we all observed the movement we cause, as an explicit reflection of our leadership effectiveness, how might we relate to one another differently? How might we expect our capitalistic organizations, governments, and institutions to behave? Would we be, and insist that our organization be, more effective and more compassionate?

Today, over fifty percent of the world's population is under the age of 35. This is mentioned here because we are, individually and collectively, leading humanity into the future. That future need not be an iteration of our past. The younger fifty percent need not be held hostage to what their elders have created – both in terms of material results and consciousness. Make no mistake, the results that we see out there are *our* collective results. There is not a "them" in positions of authority and control to look to. "They" are not the leaders who need to change their ways. A basic theme for this book is that *consciousness* is the precursor to all action, and *awareness* is its handmaiden. And, in this book awareness of consciousness will be a major domain for our inquiry.

When we consider the link between leadership and compassionate capitalism, leadership is about causing movement, and leaders of compassionate organizations focus on the quality and substance of the future. Furthermore, all leaders tend to orient themselves around the abundance of possibilities that can be attained in the future. This, we believe, is a direct consequence of consciousness. Leaders must recognize that the future of business is making the future its business. Doing so in a manner that positively impacts the planet and all who reside on it is nothing less than their moral as well as their fiduciary duty.

Business is the most pervasive force on the planet today; it touches every aspect of life, everywhere. Business must touch life in a way that is uplifting, not denigrating. Denigration derives from a philosophy of separation. This sense of separation gives rise to the pervasive belief in scarcity that drives much of the behavior of businesses and consumers alike.

We must overcome our collective attitude that we have to consume all of this quickly or it will be gone. None of this is true. We live in an abundant universe in many ways. Now, are there finite resources? Absolutely. And there are infinite possibilities for achieving results! This is why, when we pay attention to the future, it becomes our job to ensure its viability. And if that's not our focus, we will soon be out of business, both as a business entity, and as a human race.

This planet will survive us, no question about that. How we as businesses and leaders of businesses can set ourselves up as models for what's possible is a question definitely worth considering, and it is a fundamental focus of this book. Exploring how life can be lived from a perspective of abundance that informs the actions we take will have an impact relative to the wealth that we create. Capitalism is the most vital and most exuberant creator of wealth the world has known. As an economic model it has done incredible good, and the challenge today is to shift the paradigm about how we approach the creation and the stewardship of this wealth. And so begins an exploration into how we collectively own, and how we individually live out and transform the narratives that we've inherited.

Our business models today are seldom examined in the harsh light of what's being created. When we consider how these chronicles about business and leadership can be generated differently, we examine the philosophy that supports both. We examine the psychology of business, and the resulting physiology—how business physically moves, and what the consequences are.

If we change the physiology, the psychology, or the philosophy of business as elements of the existing status quo, we can then change our outcomes. We see a need to change the current state of business in the face of extremely dramatic challenges. And to paraphrase theoretical physicist Albert Einstein, solving this problem will require us to step outside the paradigms that we used to create the problem.

One of the major paradigms is our understanding of and relationship to time. We know our perceptions of reality are relative, and we also know that our notions of past, present, and future are also relative. Considered from the perspective of quantum physics, time, as we know it, does not, in fact, exist. There is only *now*. That being said, we do experience what is known as the "arrow of time" as life seems to unfold from a past through the present and into the future.

Where this becomes relevant to a new way of thinking about and conducting business is awakening to the premise that our futures have historically been created with considerable input from our pasts. It's not an exaggeration to say that, unless we become consciously intentional, our future is predestined to be very much a continuation of our past. This is not a tenable option.

We need to look toward creating the future with a different way of thinking. We need to look to a future not rooted in illusions of separation but of fundamental connection. We need to look to creating a future that recognizes an attitude of abundance (not scarcity) as the key to responsibly, utilizing and leveraging resources with sustainability and compassionate impact in mind. We need to look to building a future where business is the steward and enabler of wealth for all, not just a few.

The reason this book is so important is that it will take the legacy story of business and capitalism and use it as a solid foundation to build on as we look to the future to accelerate the paradigm shift. Then we can truly experience the future as a positive and abundant enabler of thriving for all life.

One of the places this starts is with our way of thinking about capital. Money is simply energy in motion. We're reminded of an old Bulgarian folk saying, "Money in your pocket is not meant there to stay. Money is not money until you give it away." This monetary area in today's capitalistic world typically has an inherent scarcity associated with its energy. This need not be so.

We can create significant change in the world with the wealth that's generated by capitalism. Creating massive wealth doesn't have to destroy our world, or our humanity. It actually can enhance and empower humanity to create a legacy of thriving into the future.

The mind resides in the body; it carries memories that trigger a flood of hormones and chemicals in order to create emotions and behaviors. And there's a real vibrational energy associated with those memories that is difficult to move beyond. Our minds are typically orienting us in the present with reference to our past.

So part of the challenge this book will present to you will be your willingness to take on the task of thinking bigger than your mind.

Thinking bigger than what your mind, as contained in your physical body, your body politic, and your body capitalist, has learned to be today. We need to think bigger than our minds so that we can create a different future that is abundant for all mankind.

CHAPTER 1

A Short History of Modern Capitalism—The Legacy Story

As we look deeper for the soul of capitalism, we find that,
in terms of ordinary human existence,
American capitalism doesn't appear to have one.
~ William Greider, *The Soul of Capitalism*

The structure of the story of capitalism we alluded to in the Introduction has philosophy, psychology, and physiology associated with it. It's this story, built using these three components, that we will explore. The structure of the story of capitalism, as experienced in the world today, is in a transformational process. Capitalism, we think, will be transformed by creating something more dynamic that exists, at first almost unseen within the old system, but which will break through and reshape the global economy around new values and behaviors. This is already beginning. As we move forward into this book and we begin to outline what this future looks like, it is important to examine where we come from in terms of the economic models that we embrace and the stories that we live out economically.

We won't go back to the beginning and the dawn of humans appearing on the planet, but we'll briefly examine the transition from feudalism to capitalism. Feudalism was rooted in agricultural exchange and land was the primary currency of the realm, so to speak. The philosophy of feudalism, from an economic standpoint, was rooted in obligation. This gave rise to the physiology of the serf/master relationship that continues in the worker/boss roles today. As history unfolded over the past 500 years, feudalism was replaced by essentially three types of evolving capitalism—merchant, slave, and industrial.

With the decline of feudalism in the 17th and 18th centuries, we saw the emergence of merchant, then slave capitalism, as well as all the things that were associated with them. But it was the emergence of money and credit, which didn't exist before, that was the true innovation of this period. That is, money in the sense of easily transportable *currency*, particularly gold-backed or silver-backed paper money. Credit also became something that was considered to be worthwhile; a not-so-minor point because, in fact, it was considered sinful in feudal times. This emergence into the mainstream of society and economy of credit and currency began the move toward a more active type of capitalism.

This period of early capitalism was heralded in by what we could call "The Adventurers": Christopher Columbus, Hernando de Soto, Hernán Cortés, and others. Royalty typically licensed the adventurers and they operated with extraordinary independence. Their primary mission was to extract the physical wealth of foreign lands and peoples by whatever means necessary and bring it back (less their commission, of course) to the royal treasury.

The Adventurers were eventually supplanted by "The Privateers". These included such luminaries as Sir Francis Drake, Sir Henry Morgan, and Admiral Sir John Hawkins. The charter from their respective royal sponsors enabled what was essentially legalized piracy. Interestingly, the United States continued to license privateers until the end of the 19th century. Tax records from 1790 indicate four of Boston's five top taxpayers obtained their incomes in part from privateering—including U.S. statesman and Declaration of Independence signatory John Hancock.

Beginning in the 19th century, industrial capitalism began to emerge and things changed dramatically. What we will examine in this chapter is how modern industrial capitalism has morphed and continues morphing as it just now begins to evolve into something different. As with the end of feudalism, about 500 years ago, modern-day capitalism's replacement (what we're calling *compassionate capitalism*) is being accelerated by external shocks. It will be shaped by the emergence of a new kind of human being—one who is more connected and informed than at any other time in history. A human being who is becoming more conscious and aware. And who is living in what is arguably the most peaceful and violence-free time in all recorded history.[1]

In 1776, economist and moral philosopher Adam Smith published *An Inquiry into the Nature and Causes of the Wealth of Nations*. Without going into an inordinate amount of detail, this was the first time that an economic model had been captured in print, and it was a practical way to describe how economies are structured and how they function. The core element of *The Wealth of Nations* was something that Smith called the *Invisible Hand* or *enlightened self-interest*, which essentially spoke to the notion of "You scratch my back and I'll scratch yours."

Smith posited that there was mutual benefit to be derived out of the exchange of commodities and the fostering of essentially free trade. It was enlightened self-interest that was driving and guiding capitalism at that point and it literally resulted in the wealth of nations. These nations and businesses that were actively engaged in trade became more and more prosperous. The groundwork was laid for the eventual emergence of large trading companies, such as Hudson's Bay Company, that were chartered and underwritten (and in many cases partially owned) by the state.

That gave way, in the late 19th century and the beginning of the 20th century, to the formation of the chartered corporations and the emergence of business magnates (some would say "robber barons") as exemplified by Shell Oil Company, General Motors, Lever Brothers, Siemon Company, Carnegie Corporation, R. T. Vanderbilt Holding Company, Rothschild, Rockefeller & Co., and others. These chartered corporations were created, in part, as a response to limits being imposed by legislative bodies on monarchs' powers—corporate charters bestowed monopoly rights and secured revenues free of parliamentary oversight. These early corporations (for example, British East India Company,

Dutch East India Company, and Hudson's Bay Company) were used to create some of the earliest colonial settlements and, truth be told, were essentially legally sanctioned and protected crime syndicates.

Their behavior became so rapacious that in *The General Theory of Employment, Interest and Money,* economist John Maynard Keynes took the position that state intervention is necessary to moderate boom-and-bust cycles of economic activity that are present when free trade and free markets are left unfettered.[2] Keynesian economics held sway for much of the first half of the 20th century and Keynes was certainly considered one of the preeminent economists of the early 20th century.

Near the middle of the 20th century, philosopher Ayn Rand appeared on the scene and wrote the influential books *The Fountainhead* and *Atlas Shrugged.* In a collection of essays, *Capitalism: The Unknown Ideal,* published in 1966 with Allen Greenspan, Nathaniel Branden and Robert Hessen, she posits that capitalism is the only morally valid sociopolitical system because it allows people to be free to act in their rational self-interest.[3] The keyword in her philosophy is *rational,* as opposed to the *enlightened* self-interest or mutual benefit that Adam Smith championed. Rand's work began to move the philosophy and the psychology of business from a focus on mutual benefit to one of rational self-interest. This was a major shift in the way that economic activity was viewed.

This move was abetted by the work of economist Milton Friedman, winner of the Nobel Memorial Prize in Economic Sciences in 1976, who essentially replaced Keynes as the leading economist in the last half of the 20th century. In his book, *Capitalism and Freedom,* Friedman postulated that it was the social responsibility of a business to increase its profits. That is a major statement that put Americans on a track, as a capitalist economic society, to orient their business activities not for the higher good of society in general, but for the self-interest of the organization and its shareholders.

Today, although not explicit in law, the principle that the legal and ethical obligation of management is to place financial returns for shareholders above all other interests has become deeply embedded in case law and legal culture. Under current U.S. law, publicly traded corporations are held to be a legal "person" but are also excused and/or prohibited from exercising the ethical sensibility and moral responsibility normally expected of a natural-born, emotionally mature adult—the absence of which is the definition of sociopathic behavior.

What we have come to experience is that irresponsibility in the pursuit of profit is what makes capitalism succeed. The philosophical context espoused by Friedman and Rand and embraced by business and business leaders has created a physiology hallmarked by behaviors in which businesses (and increasingly individuals) act as if they are not responsible for consequences, but only for the production and consumption of those things that allow our rational self-interests to be realized—profit and shareholder return being the most obvious measure of success. It's a highly focused and extremely myopic orientation.

This trajectory has moved us in our collective experience of capitalism to a point where, from our perspective, it's no longer tenable or sustainable as it is currently practiced. We believe we are now at a point in history where capitalism is again being transformed into something more dynamic. There are forces that are becoming more and more visible that will reshape our economies around new altruistic values and behaviors.

Before we explore that concept, let's look at what we might be leaving behind—both the good and the bad.

Capitalism Has Been VERY Good

Nations became wealthier through unfettered trade that was enabled by, and that coincided with, the emergence of money and credit, both of which were required in order to create a relatively free market system. What arose from this was a broader spectrum of people, different from the serfs of feudal economies that came to be known as the merchant class or now as the middle class. As they began to acquire more and more wealth, this class moved away from land being its sole determinant of wealth. Instead, wealth was becoming a consequence of trade, and, as it did so, wealth became more and more widely distributed.

If you consider the world's wealth about 500 years ago, almost all of it was based on land holdings. But if we examine the Forbes list of the wealthiest individuals today,[4] from Bill Gates to Carlos Slim Helu to Warren Buffett to Amancio Ortega to Larry Ellison, their wealth has little to do with any land holdings (or any materially "real" assets at all). The consequences of this shift are inescapable. If your wealth depended on the quality of your land holdings, as a land owner you'd naturally care more about the land, the actual earth. You'd actually feel more connected to the source of your wealth. This is not the case with today's business leaders.

Because economies (and businesses) are now driven by information, service, and speculative value, we wonder how that plays into creating the increasing dystopia of disconnection and disengagement that many experience in the world today. Many business leaders tend to disregard the social consequences of doing business in pursuit of a less tangibly sourced wealth as "just the cost of doing business." We aren't going back to the gold standard or to wealth based on "real" holding, and this is why we have to shift the paradigm toward different things, such as people, life, and earth, and redefine the nature of value creation beyond just the accumulation of money.

As we moved into the modern capitalist age, where we saw the emergence of industrial capitalism (which began in the late 1700s, early 1800s) we saw the emergence of trade unions and collective bargaining. These were part of that particular style of capitalism. Ayn Rand hadn't come onto the stage yet, and the Invisible Hand described in *The Wealth of Nations* was still in play. The emergence of trade unions and the appearance of child labor laws were things that needed to be addressed for the good of society, not just the corporation stakeholders as defined by the investing class or the owner class. These things became the admirable parts of the capitalist legacy.

24

The feudal model was based on agriculture and was partially defined by the serf/master relationship. But as we moved into a capitalist model that freed the serfs from the land and from indentureship, we witnessed a collision with environmental concerns as more serfs left to become members of the emerging merchant class. Then there was a massive external shock, the Black Plague, which killed an estimated 75–200 million people in the 1300s. This was followed by a demographic shock, with too few people to work the land.

This created a labor shortage that forced the technological innovations that underpinned and accelerated the rise of merchant capitalism. Commerce required greater regulation and innovation, and this occurred through the emergence of accounting and printing as tradable wealth came into play. Because we could now navigate according to longitude and latitude, faster and larger ships were built. One of the consequences of this was that mining became more pervasive, which set the stage for a migration to industrial capitalism.

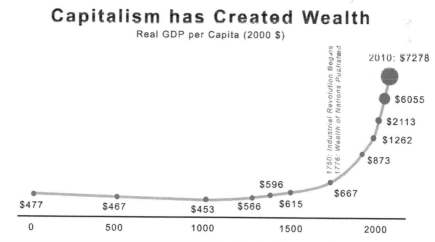

Capitalism has Created Wealth
Real GDP per Capita (2000 $)

Sources: www.visualizingeconomics.com; Angus Maddison University of Groningen; www.prb.org; www.worldbank.org

(Originally published in *Conscious Capitalism: Liberating the Heroic Spirit of Business* by Raj Sisodia and John Mackey. Adapted and used by permission from Raj Sisodia.)

At the time of the Black Plague in the 14th century, per capita income was about $450 (adjusted to 2000 dollars). When Columbus landed in North America in 1492, the average income was $596. At the beginning of the Industrial Revolution in the mid-1700s, per capita income climbed almost geometrically. By 2010, per capita income had climbed to more than $7,000. Prior to that, it was flat-lined for almost **1,500 years**. It's only in the past 500 years, with the advent of feudalism and the subsequent evolution through merchant capitalism and toward industrial capitalism, that per capita income gained ground dramatically.

Make no mistake, capitalism has been an incredible creator of wealth and has radically transformed the living experience of most people on the planet in a fundamental way. One of the great benefits of wealth creation is the natural impact that greater wealth has on poverty. In the mid-1800s, the percentage of the world population living on less than a dollar a day was almost 95 percent. But in 2003 (in adjusted dollars) it was about 5 percent.[5] Nobel Peace Prize Laureate Professor Muhammad Yunus predicts that by close to 2020, we will have eradicated what we call extreme poverty (those individuals living on less than a dollar a day). This is a direct consequence of the wealth that is created by the capitalist economic model.

Capitalism is Ending Poverty

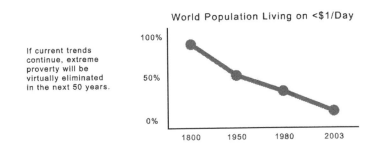

World Population Living on <$1/Day

If current trends continue, extreme poverty will be virtually eliminated in the next 50 years.

Source: World Bank (2003 dollars)

(Originally published in *Conscious Capitalism: Liberating the Heroic Spirit of Business* by Raj Sisodia and John Mackey. Adapted and used by permission from Raj Sisodia.)

What else has capitalism fostered that we consider as good? People don't always recognize this in large part because of the ratings and profit focus of many news outlets. Contrary to all the violence reported daily in the news media, today we actually live in the single most peaceful time in human history. Murder rates are 30 times lower than they were in the Middle Ages.[6] Violence against women has dropped dramatically and significant interstate wars have not occurred since World War II.[7] One of the major reasons for this is the growth of commerce. With trade, there are opportunities for positive-sum exchange, where all benefit, as opposed to zero-sum plunder. Trading partners just want to take care of one another. This goes directly back to Adam Smith and the Invisible Hand of enlightened self-interest.

Then there is the "Flynn effect", named for political scientist James Flynn, who first documented that there has been an average decadal three-point increase in intelligence, as measured by IQ, going back to the late-1800s when IQ tests were first administered in large scale. Generationally, this represents about a 12-point increase. We are becoming "smarter". The Flynn effect has been documented in more than 30 countries in both developed and developing parts of the world. We are becoming more intelligent as a species and part of the reason is due to healthier diets and greater access to healthcare that is the positive consequence of having greater wealth. Capitalism's wealth creation propensity arguably provides what is required in order to improve our ability to reach the creative potential of being human.

Globally, we are also sending our children to school for longer periods of time—3.2 years in 1950 and 5.3 years in 1980. This is due to a number of factors, not the least of which is a realization of the economic impact of education. According to *The Journal of Monetary Economics,* the rates of return on economic output for each additional year of schooling range from 5 percent to 12 percent.

Most important, capitalism has fostered an increase in awareness that is part of education. We'll explore this in more depth in a later section, but it's worth noting here that an increase in awareness increases our choice-making capacity by illuminating the previously unseen and/ or unnoticed choices available to us. People today have more choices available to them than ever before. Part of our challenge with an increase in awareness is the ability to be more discerning and more cogent of the long-term impact of our choices. There is hope that we will be able to meet this challenge based on the simple fact that our general awareness of our world is increasing and this is, in part, directly attributable to the emergence of capitalism on the world stage.

All of these outcomes derive from modern capitalism . . . from wealth creation, to poverty eradication and violence reduction, to increased access to education, and to increasing overall intelligence. Our increasing awareness of the different choices available to us is also due to greater access to information at instantaneous speeds, which is becoming ubiquitous. There are now more active phone numbers in the world than there are people—more than 7.3 billion as of this writing. Facebook exceeded the billion-member mark in October 2012. In 2015, Twitter averaged 280 million active users. Alternative social networks such as Webo, Snapchat, WhatsApp, Line, and LinkedIn continue to emerge, each with millions of members. According to the United Nations Broadband Commission, almost 60 percent of all people on the planet will have access to the Internet by the year 2020.

Facebook through Internet.org (drones and satellite constellation), Google through Project Loon (helium balloons), and Qualcomm and Virgin through OneWeb (satellite constellation) made strides in 2015 to provide global connectivity to every human on Earth at speeds exceeding 1 megabit per second. Google Loon actually deployed working balloons and, as of this writing, OneWeb closed $500M in capital to build its system.

Globally, the population on Earth will grow from three to eight billion connected humans, adding five billion new consumers to the global economy during the next five years. These "rising billions" represent tens of trillions of new dollars flowing into the global economy.

And they are not coming online like early adopters did 20 years ago with a 9600-baud modem. They're coming online with a 1 Mbps and faster connections and access to the world's information on Google, cloud 3D printing, Amazon Web Services, artificial intelligence with Watson and AlphaGo, crowdfunding, crowdsourcing, and more.

This degree of interconnectedness is unprecedented in human history and is a phenomenon of modern day capitalism. We believe that this is leading to an emergence of consciousness that is transforming us based on the fact that we are more connected and interdependent than we have ever realized. This emerging collective consciousness leads to the possibility for us becoming more aware of our connection to and with *all* other things. It's this awareness of connection that compels us to position *compassion* as the foundation for all business activity.

Capitalism Has Also Been VERY Bad

With all positives, there are concomitant negatives with which we need to contend. This is one way that we progress: What once worked no longer works and, in fact, it might be extremely destructive if continued. Looking at "the bad" with anything can compel us to pause and make different choices. If you quantitatively and qualitatively examine the challenges that we see arising due to modern capitalism, such as increasing wealth disparity, disengaged employees, environmental degradation, unsustainable debt-based consumerism, and a culture pervasively focused on "me," we can appreciate the need to make significant changes *now*.

The significance of identifying the bad is that it signals the "system" that we have both the impetus and the ability to make changes to how we are currently conducting ourselves. Imagine being in a feudal economy 600 years ago. There would have come a time where we'd have to question the current state. We'd likely come to believe that if we didn't create more wealth, if we didn't have poverty reduction, and, more important, if we didn't stop interstate and interpersonal violence, the status quo would be our great undoing.

Today, if we allow wealth disparity to continue to grow, the number of disengaged employees to grow, environmental degradation to grow, and a continued focus on separation as the norm, we will have also ensured our destruction as a species. We will always have the Freudian and Darwinian challenges of survival, and we must continually learn to leverage our awareness to turn these negatives into positives and take control of this transformation, just the same as we always have.

The thrust of this book is not to demonize capitalism; indeed, an incredible amount of good can be leveraged out of it if we can connect capitalism to a spiritual "soul". As a species, we are raising both our consciousness and awareness to a point where we can make some choices that are not driven simply by survival needs. One of the benefits of capitalism is that it has moved much of humankind up psychologist Abraham Maslow's famous hierarchy of needs from physical survival through psychological belonging to the more altruistic self-actualization needs. It's also important to recognize that, as currently practiced, the capitalist system functions without a soul or a heart. Life will not and cannot continue to support such a system. Life has soul. Life has heart.

The human condition is learned. As we have become wealthier and more interdependent while ignoring how we are increasingly, sensationally separate from our environment, we set up a tension that can't be ignored. This, we think, is an important realization. The "bad" in capitalism is the consequence of destructive competition, which is rooted in a learned misunderstanding of a notion attributed to naturalist Charles Darwin—the survival of the fittest—an assumption that is rooted in a Cartesian philosophy of duality and separation. What Darwin actually said was that it was the most adaptable that would survive.

Adaptability is rooted in connection, and connection requires— demands even—cooperation in order to be sustained. Cooperation, not unbridled competition, enhances the chances of survival. Cooperation makes the pie bigger. Competition tends to shrink a pie and becomes destructive over the long term. Survival of the adaptable is based on cooperation and collaboration, not on dog eat dog competition. Cooperation is rooted in connection, not separation.

A relevant example in the legal research space highlights what occurred in the pre-chasm of the Internet (the word "chasm" as used here refers to the deep difference that exists between the market of early adopters and the mainstream, and the difficulty of bringing a product that is successful in the former, to the latter). When accessing legal information online, there were two big players: LexisNexis and West Publishing. This was a pure, one-on-one competitive space which effectively functioned to educate the market about the effective utilization of the Internet for research. Today research has become one of the biggest businesses in the world. Google now does the same thing that LexisNexis and West Publishing did, where each started with a Boolean language based on a logic system, then evolved to natural language searching to access the databases they owned. The information that was searched was limited at that time to statutes, laws, and secondary materials, and was contained in the respective databases.

In retrospect, we can see that Google leveraged its optimization tool and because of an emerging cooperation among competitors, this space grew, not only economically, but in terms of greater and more timely access for everyone. This created an entire industry that generated billions of dollars in revenue and continues to do so. The real value, however, was that we became increasingly connected and far more able to access information of all kinds.

The great takeaway here is that if there hadn't been collaborative/cooperative competition in this search space, it wouldn't have created the vast opportunities we have today. The cooperative focus was on educating the market about how important it is to do research online in order to maximize effectiveness, and then to compete to do it better than anyone else. In the end, the pie grows and everybody wins.

There's something interesting about the LexisNexis dynamic: If we back up even further today and think about what is the largest information product in the world, it's not Google. Wikipedia has the distinction of being the largest global information product. It is created and maintained by volunteers and it's free to use. It eliminated the printed encyclopedia, and the advertising industry estimates it cost them $3 billion a year in lost revenue. We are in an information age and an emerging digital economy that is poorly understood. It will be fascinating to see how this evolves and how it actually impacts and disrupts existing businesses. We can do this either accidentally or mindfully. Unwarranted competition will only keep the pie small.

Adaptability almost guarantees disruption if it's allowed to take root. This is both the cost and the reward. The "bad" here is that resisting disruption—protecting the status quo—is one of the hallmarks of today's capitalist organizations. They are so entrenched in their markets, invested in their revenue streams, and beholden to their shareholders, the imperative to respond to innovative challenges from outsiders is typically done by calling for increased regulation and enforcement of the status quo—the antithesis of cooperation and adaptability.

The largest transportation company today is Uber (with a market cap of $62 billion at this writing)—but Uber doesn't own any vehicles. The largest hotelier is AirBnB—but it doesn't own any properties. The largest energy providers of tomorrow will not be utilities; they will be micro grids that are independent of any single distribution or production source. Adaptability based on cooperation doesn't diminish the value of competition and it MUST diminish the attraction of mindless and inappropriate competition rooted in philosophies of dominance, maintaining status quo, and the associated win/lose psychologies. We will always have companies going out of business, but how can we do this in a way that minimizes the consequences of disruption? That's one of the things that we will examine as we look at capitalism through the lens of compassion.

What's really so bad about our current capitalistic model? In a word: consumption. There are essentially five areas we can (and will) explore that highlight the disastrous consequences of how business based on ever-increasing consumption is being conducted today:

1. Rampant consumerism
2. Employee disengagement
3. Wealth disparity
4. Environmental degradation
5. Poverty of meaning

Rampant Consumerism

Our current economic model is completely driven by a need for continual growth that is fueled by consumption. Not just any type of consumption, mind you, but an ever-increasing and never-ending consumption that is necessary as *the* fuel required to drive this ravenous economic engine. How do we pay for this need for ever-increasing consumption when wages are flat and 95 percent of the wealth being created goes to the top 1 percent? Debt is the answer.

Debt finances growth. Global credit doubled from $57 trillion to $109 trillion from the years 2000 to 2010. With the requirement to continue to feed this beast, according to the World Economic Forum, the total global credit has to double to more than $210 trillion by the year 2020 in order to provide the necessary credit driven growth just to *preserve current gross domestic product (GDP) levels.* There is currently not that much money available on the planet! This is clearly an unsustainable model when examined in this context.

Global stock of debt outstanding,
$ trillion, constant 2013 exchange rates

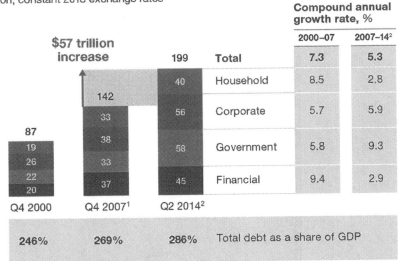

			Compound annual growth rate, %	
			2000–07	2007–14[2]
199		Total	7.3	5.3
40		Household	8.5	2.8
56		Corporate	5.7	5.9
58		Government	5.8	9.3
45		Financial	9.4	2.9

$57 trillion increase

87 — 19, 26, 22, 20

142 — 33, 38, 33, 37

Q4 2000   Q4 2007[1]   Q2 2014[2]

| 246% | 269% | 286% | Total debt as a share of GDP |

[1]Figures do not sum to total, because of rounding.
[2]Q2 2014 data for advanced economies and China; Q4 2013 data for other developing countries.

Source: Bank for International Settlements; Haver Analytics; International Monetary Fund *World Economic Outlook*; national sources; McKinsey Global Institute analysis

The 2008 economic crash wiped 13 percent of global production off the map and it wiped out 20 percent of global trade. Global GDP growth became negative about 2008, on a scale where anything now below about 3 percent annual growth is counted as a recession. And that is not a sustainable figure. When you add to this the consequence of wealth disparity, things really begin to get interesting. In real dollars, of all the new growth created from 2009 to 2012, the top 1 percent of the population took 95 percent of all new wealth created in that timeframe.

This wealth disparity causes a social dynamic that is not sustainable. It's being evidenced in the way that trust is measured toward big business. People just don't trust big business any longer. In fact, according to a 2015 Gallup survey people's trust of big business ranks only above Congress— which is saying quite a bit—and one of the consequences of this is the ever-increasing phenomenon of a disengaged employees within these businesses.

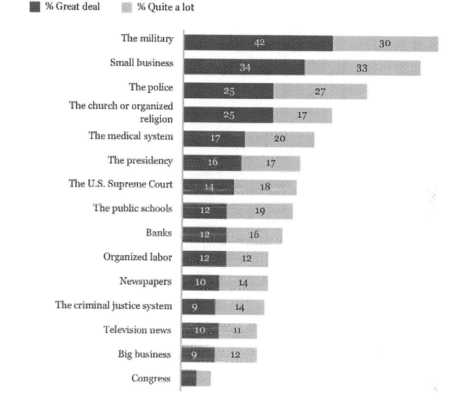

■ % Great deal   ▨ % Quite a lot

	% Great deal	% Quite a lot
The military	42	30
Small business	34	33
The police	25	27
The church or organized religion	25	17
The medical system	17	20
The presidency	16	17
The U.S. Supreme Court	14	18
The public schools	12	19
Banks	12	16
Organized labor	12	12
Newspapers	10	14
The criminal justice system	9	14
Television news	10	11
Big business	9	12
Congress		

GALLUP

Employee Disengagement

There's a common business saying: "Our people are our greatest assets." Another version of it reads: "Our people are our greatest resources." If we examine the language used in either of these statements (*assets* and *resources*), we discover the roots of a considerable problem. Assets are depreciated over time on a balance sheet for tax purposes. If employers are treating people as assets, there's an implicit promise that suggests employees too will be depreciated over time.

And resources are intended to be used up. Idle resources are anathema in any organization. If people are treated and feel like they are resources, they ultimately come to believe and experience that they're being used up… depleted of their value. It's not in any way surprising that the experience of many in organizations, and this goes directly to the phenomenon of emotional engagement, is that people understand that they're being depreciated as they are being used up. They experience being disposable (depreciated) when their "useful life" is reached (they become redundant or expensive). They also experience being used for no meaningful purpose, other than the profit-driving mechanism of most businesses.

This results in disengaged or uninspired employees, which carries an immense cost to business. It results in people not paying attention to what needs to be focused on. Some of the specific consequences are that people don't raise their hands and object to work processes that result in environmental degradation or safety concerns. As an example of this, you have the old Pinto car case (exploding fuel tanks), where Ford weighed the actual value of future litigation against the cost of recalling and repairing something that they knew had the potential to harm human beings. Ford did an economic analysis and determined that it would rather pay the lawsuits for killing people than actually fixing the car.

Similarly, General Motors ignored problems with its ignition systems that carried essentially the same safety risks. Yet another example includes big tobacco covering up the research that it knew existed relative to planned ways to make tobacco more addictive, despite its known carcinogenic effects. More recently there is evidence that oil companies buried internal studies showing the environmentally harmful consequences of burning fossil fuels and that Takata ignored data about faulty airbags that have resulted in numerous deaths. All in deference to profit.

Today, the dynamics of capitalism implicitly encourage businesses in the tobacco industry to aggressively market cigarettes in underdeveloped countries to foster continued consumption, all while getting those populations addicted to nicotine. Perversely, this provides a growing market for medicines and healthcare to save people from the diseases that were knowingly created.

These issues revolve around a misunderstanding about the notion of the survival of the fittest. It's not the fittest—the fiercest competitors—who survive, but (in our view) the most adaptable and the most cooperative. A lot of what we're describing about tobacco, oil, defective vehicles, or the off-shoring of toxic waste are examples of the primary driver of capitalism today, which is based on consumption in order to fuel growth of revenue and profit. This is an unconscionable travesty.

Wealth Disparity

Our current capitalist model is at the root of much social unrest. A prime example is the dramatic increase in wealth disparity. It's not an accident that the Occupy movement gained so much traction without a clearly defined agenda. There was just a sense of outrage fueled by a difficult-to-identify knowing that something was wrong. And, that *something* is much deeper than a simple gap in wealth. It is the consequence of modern capitalism's unblinking focus on profit.

In part, this does speak to the 1 percent / 99 percent wealth-disparity dynamic that is a function of the way that capital has become the supreme measure of success. The acquisition and accumulation of capital has become the major metric by which organizations and individuals declare whether they are successful or not. There is not a problem with this on its face. However, when this becomes the *primary* focus of business activity the results are toxic. The *acquisition* of wealth is vastly different than the *accumulation* of wealth and the two have become toxically intertwined. Wealth is essentially energy that has the power to create and to destroy. It is in this energetic sense that the acquisition and circulation of wealth enables the creation of many things. As such, it is a worthy aspiration. Apple is the most valuable company on the planet. According to its 1st Quarter 2016 earnings report it has accumulated a cash hoard in excess of $216 Billion. How that amount of accumulated energy is used is important. When acquisition of wealth begins to accumulate with no creative circulatory outlet there is a problem. The greater the accumulation of any form of energy, the greater the danger when the dam bursts — the resulting "flow" is often highly destructive.

In April of 2016 Iceland's Prime Minister Sigmundur Davíð Gunnlaugsso was forced to resign over revelations made in the release of the so called Panama Papers that exposed the secret offshore accounts and shell corporations set up by some of the wealthiest people on the planet to shelter their money and avoid taxation. Contrast this to The Giving Pledge[8] started by Warren Buffet and Bill Gates. This is a campaign to encourage the wealthy people of the world to contribute their *accumulated* wealth to philanthropic causes. It is specifically focused on billionaires or those who would be billionaires if not for their giving. As of March 2016, 142 individuals and/or couples had signed the pledge to give the majority of their net worth to philanthropy, either during their lifetime or upon their death.

The United States today has the worst income inequality in the developed world – an inequality not seen since the time of the Robber Barons of the 19th century.

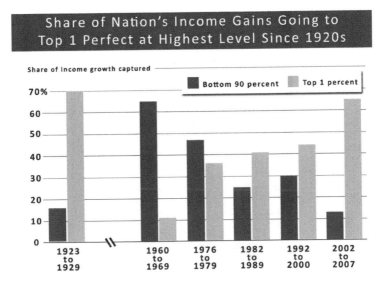

Source: CBPP calculations based on data from Piketty and Saez

In fact, it may be more unbalanced than at any time since before the Revolutionary War when the U.S. middle class – the foundation of the American Dream – was arguably far more prevalent than it is today.

We need to examine how this plays out in the way business organizations conduct themselves and, more importantly, the societal costs that this inequality spawns.

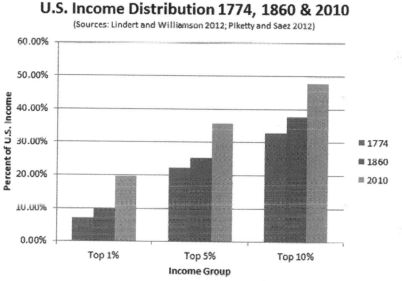

U.S. Income Distribution 1774, 1860 & 2010
(Sources: Lindert and Williamson 2012; Piketty and Saez 2012)

One example is what can only be called the return of "Debtor Prisons". This phenomenon affects only the poor, which is an increasingly large segment of the population. Although the U.S. and many states abolished debtor prisons in the 1830s and the Supreme Court has made clear in at least three separate rulings that debtor prisons are unconstitutional, state and local courts routinely ignore this. Today, fifteen states allow courts, through loopholes (such as failure to appear at a court hearing) to existing law to incarcerate the poor for failure to pay even minor fines. Not coincidentally, these states also have the highest incarceration rates in the U.S. Additionally, felony offenders who have completed their prison sentences will often find themselves back in jail when they can't pay fees and fines owed because they weren't able to earn money while incarcerated. This may not be an "accident".

The U.S. incarcerates more people per capita than any other nation on the planet. Its imprisonment rate per capita is about 320% higher than China's and is 50% higher than Russia's. And, this is not the result of higher crime rates. The U.S. simply imprisons more types of criminal offenders—the vast proportion of whom are poor and non-white. Part of the reason? Private prison companies and the *profit* available to them for running their "business" at as close to maximum capacity as possible. In 2010, two prison corporations made three billion dollars in profit. Approximately ten percent of all U.S. prisoners are housed in private prisons. And at least 65% of these private prisons have contracts with states that include quotas (called occupancy guarantee provisions) that the state is obligated to meet to make sure that they stay full and don't incur a penalty fee if occupancy rates fall below the guaranteed levels. The states of Arizona, Louisiana, Oklahoma and Virginia are locked into contracts requiring between 95% and 100% occupancy! These contract clauses obviously incentivize keeping prisons full, which runs counter to public policy goals of reducing prison populations. One could be excused if they were to assume that policy decisions should be based on creating and maintaining a just criminal justice system designed to protect the public interest, not one that is based on ensuring corporate profits. Unfortunately, capitalism today insures no such outcome.

Another consequence of growing wealth disparity, particularly in the United States, is the consolidation of the power to influence economic legislation and regulation that is linked to wealth accumulation. In 1982, Judge Harold Green presided over the antitrust case (United States vs. AT&T) that broke up the AT&T monopoly. Today, one could legitimately claim it has been reconstituted. The same with the old Standard Oil. Monsanto has essentially a monopoly on seed production in the world and the major Wall Street firms that are "Too Big to Fail" have effectively funded (lobbied) for the repel of and/or undermined enforcement of laws regulating their activities. To quote Adam Smith from *Wealth of Nations*, "...the cruelest of our revenue laws, I will venture to affirm, are mild and gentle in comparison of some of those which the clamor of our merchants and manufacturers has extorted from the legislature for the support of their own absurd and oppressive monopolies. Like the laws of Draco, these laws may be said to be all written in blood."

Modern capitalism's all-consuming love affair with profits has poisoned the well. The consequences of wealth inequality are social in nature and toxic in the extreme. The problem with wealth inequality isn't just that wealth is concentrated in the pocketbooks of the one percent. It is that commerce is not played out on a level field, access to information necessary to make good decisions becomes constrained (before YouTube appeared, all media in the world was controlled by 10 CEOs), and services that are rightfully intended for the public good (such as prisons, healthcare, broadcast television, and education) end up becoming for-profit businesses that are incentivized to engage in practices that compromise – sometimes drastically – the well-being of all of society.

Money is a form of energy. It needs to flow in order to be useful. When flow ceases, problems arise. We can think of this in physical terms using the body as a metaphor. Money is the metaphoric analog to your blood. If your blood doesn't flow, you will have a problem. This isn't conjecture. It's fact. You will die. The same is true with the economy. The hoarding or accumulation of money represents a cessation in it's flow. When the flow is constricted, parts of the body begin to contract and will eventually die. All other consequences of wealth disparity pale in comparison to the import of this fact.

Environmental Degradation

It's obvious to all that we live on a planet that's our only source of the materials necessary for life to exist as we know it, and that provides our species with our existential place in the cosmos. Our current economic model has put this planet and everything on it in extreme jeopardy.

There was recently a report released on the website overshootday. org that addresses the utilization of resources on Earth. According to the data cited, we have actually exceeded the Earth's capacity to renew itself in terms of the amount of resources that we now use. This is called global overshoot and it's critically important. Global overshoot occurs when humanity's annual demand for the goods and services that the earth can provide—fruits and vegetables, meat, fish, wood, raw resources— exceeds what Earth's ecosystems can renew in a year. Overshoot means we are drawing down the planet's principal rather than living off its annual interest. This leads to a depletion of Earth's life-supporting natural capital and a buildup of carbon dioxide in the atmosphere.[9] Stated simply, global overshoot occurs when human demand exceeds the supply of the natural ecosystem. We've gotten to that point. We used more of the earth's resources by August 21, 2015, than the Earth was capable of regenerating that year. This timeframe is getting shorter and shorter each year as we use continually more than the Earth can regenerate. This is an enormous problem that is, to a significant degree, a consequence of current business activities.

A simple riddle helps put this in perspective. There is a pond (it doesn't matter how big the pond is) and in this pond is a lily pad. This is a special lily pad that doubles in size every day. On the 40th day, the lily pad fills the whole pond. On what day did the lily pad fill half the pond? The correct answer is the 39th day. The process is exponential and we are rapidly approaching the 39th day.

The exponential growth required to continue to fuel the current economic model is unsustainable. The planet went into overshoot in the early 1970s. Human activity requires from the ecosystem more than the Earth can produce just to sustain the level of human activity that we're generating today. In business terms, we are significantly over budget. We're drawing down on reserves that we don't have the ability to replenish any longer. We have used the earth's ecosystem as a credit card and have not paid anything significant to retire the debt. And, the "bank" is about to cancel the card.

Poverty of Meaning

There's an interesting concept posited by Indian economist and philosopher Amartya Sen, winner of the 1998 Nobel Memorial Prize in Economic Sciences. He has defined poverty as the situation where "people lack the means to appear in public without shame."[10] Essentially, he is describing a poverty of meaning that is borne out of economic activity focused solely on consumption, and that leaves a society bereft of soul and heart. And, it is driving ever-increasing consumerism in an attempt to appease the emptiness felt when meaning is absent. The illusion foisted on consumers is that life will be more meaningfully experienced and lived if one has the latest and best of what's being sold.

We don't need more stuff, but we think we do. Part of the dysfunction that we're running into, part of the malaise, has to do with an increase in this poverty of meaning. The experience of a life devoid of true and uplifting meaning is a huge consequence of the way our economic model is structured, causing us to be reliant on ever increasing consumption for our sense of happiness.

The philosophy of separation fostered by French philosopher, mathematician, and scientist René Descartes and his contemporaries has placed the source of "happiness" outside of oneself. Dubbed the father of modern Western philosophy, Descartes' famous saying, "Cogito ergo sum"—I think, therefore I am—has had enormous ramifications. The structure of Descartes' thinking as evidenced by his famous phrase places form (I think) before consciousness (I am). French philosopher Jean-Paul Sartre examined the statement and concluded that "The voice that says 'I Am' is not the same voice that thinks." This is not a simple semantic or linguistic distinction. It's that deeper, behind-the-scenes voice that gives rise to the notion of a universal, pervasive soul or spirit that is connected to all.

The subject/object dichotomy rooted in Cartesian philosophy keeps us separate from what we observe and experience. And, if we experience

"I am" as separate from who we intrinsically are, we have a continuously empty hole that needs filling. Today, many attempt to fill it from outside themselves. Increasingly enabled by incredibly sophisticated marketing techniques, we have come to believe that life is meaningless without the latest and greatest new gizmo.

The cost of this is profound. According to a study recently released by the U.S. Centers for Disease Control and Prevention (CDC), suicide in the United States has surged to the highest levels in nearly 30 years.[11] Katherine Hempstead, senior adviser for health care at the Robert Wood Johnson Foundation said, "It's really stunning to see such a large increase in suicide rates affecting virtually every age group." According to Robert Putnam, professor of public policy at Harvard, "This is part of the larger emerging pattern of evidence of the links between poverty, hopelessness and health."

The Reasons for Bad

Let's look at where this "bad" comes from. We can trace it to René Descartes and Blaise Pascal, along with many of their contemporaries, when a philosophy was defined that focused on a separation of humans from nature. Descartes' admonition of "I think, therefore I am," was the verbal declaration that signified a break from a more holistic experience of humankind participating as a partner in life with the rest of the ecosystem. Much of subsequent Western philosophy is a response to his writings.

The Cartesian dictum posited that we are not just separate from nature, we are also the masters of nature—we have to be if we are to control the external which, as seen through this lens, is the source of our happiness. Separateness ultimately creates, then reinforces, a scarcity consciousness and, not coincidentally this scarcity is what drives markets. Taken to a logical conclusion, the Cartesian notion of "I think, therefore I am," has fostered a sense of entitlement that reinforces competition at the expense of cooperation, consumption at the expense of sustainability, and irresponsibility at the expense of integrity.

Also contributing to the bad is the fact that the capitalist market *system* is fundamentally different from capitalism. This is not a minor point or a simple semantic distinction. The addition of the suffix *ism* changes the game. A market system is any systematic process enabling many market players to bid and ask: Helping bidders and sellers interact and make deals. It is not just the price mechanism, but the entire system of regulation, qualification, credentials, reputations, and clearing that surrounds that mechanism and makes it operate in a social context.[14]

A capitalist market system was ideally envisioned as being based on free trade, informed by a moral center. It's not an accident that Adam Smith wrote *The Theory of Moral Sentiment (1759)* before he wrote *An Inquiry into the Nature and Causes of the Wealth Of Nations (1776)*. The Invisible Hand of enlightened self-interest espoused in the *Wealth of Nations* was *The Theory of Moral Sentiment* in action. It was envisioned as a capitalist market system with both heart and soul. The fact that the two books were written 17 years apart may be coincidental but it appears that the link between the two books is what Ayn Rand, Milton Friedman, and Alan Greenspan missed.

All *isms* eventually become dogmas. *Isms* represent the body of critically unexamined thought…*isms* are seldom questioned by their adherents. The philosophical and psychological underpinnings of all *isms* that retain vitality over time are typically considered by its adherents as inviolate "truth". We worship nothing so much as certainty even if that certainty slowly creates a prison around us.

Capitalism, like other *isms*, is an ideology. This one is economically based but it's an ideology nonetheless (and in its current form approaches dogma). As with most words, there is more than one definition for the word ideology. The one that is most useful here is "A set of ideas proposed by the dominant class of society such as the elite to all members of society."[13] It is a useful definition because as the capitalist market system took root, significant wealth began to be generated. And as can be expected, with human nature being what it was and still is, for many the game become one of seeing who could "corner the market" in order to accrue more wealth. The ideal became corrupt. A truly free market guided by an enlightened hand faded into the distance as a naïve anachronism.

Although a truly free market system in and of itself does not require external regulating because it, by definition, is self-regulating, it is almost impossible to identify one that actually exists. Indeed, nature is probably the only example of a truly free market system. It's the absence of heart and soul—the absence of a sense of connection provided by a moral sentiment—that calls forth a need for regulation. It's the all-too-visible hand of rational self-interest espoused by Ayn Rand and Milton Friedman that serves as the driver of today's economic activity. It is this, as opposed to the Invisible Hand of enlightened self-interest guided by the *The Theory of Moral Sentiment*, that has caused much of what we are now faced with needing to rectify. Otherwise, the system we created to sustain us may irreversibly end up killing us.

CHAPTER 2

A Future History of Compassionate Capitalism

"The things that will destroy us are: politics without
principle; pleasure without conscience; wealth without work;
knowledge without character; business without morality; science
without humanity; and worship without sacrifice."
~ Mahatma Gandhi

Capitalism has veered into an ultra-competitive dynamic, when cooperation is actually what is required to ensure wealth and thriving, long-term success. As we saw in the previous chapter, there are numerous examples of inappropriate competition wreaking havoc.

One of the things that we know to be true is that when two competing paradigms collide, the one paradigm that has the capacity to absorb the other will be the one that dominates. Examples of this are scattered throughout history. For example, Copernicus proposing that the Earth orbits the sun; the Earth being round, not flat; quantum physics encompassing Newtonian physics; and digitization in the form of 3-D printing replacing traditional manufacturing, and ultimately more and more machines replacing humans in the job market.

We think that a compassionate capitalism paradigm not only can but must absorb and supplant the current model of capitalism as it is currently being practiced. There's a mechanism for understanding how this occurs and how what we have in front of us now will not be sustainable in the long term. The possibility to absorb what has gone before is, in essence, a form of Darwinism. Not in the sense of "survival of the fittest" but in the sense of survival being the prerogative of the one who will adapt most effectively.

We believe we can find a way with this new paradigm—the compassionate capitalism paradigm (which includes conscious capitalism)—that can lead us to mindfully collaborate with the existing system and move to a more holistic, a more generative, and a more thriving worldview that will have the power to drive decisions and behaviors in ways that are less myopic and more consistent with our compassionate worldview.

Under the current paradigm, capitalism will not survive unless consumption continues to drive and fuel it. The problem, as we've seen, is that ever-increasing consumption is a non-sustainable way of addressing the need for continued economic growth. It quickly runs aground on the reality of a scarcity of material resources that we're progressively encountering on the planet—not the least of which will be a lack of potable water and a diminishing food supply due to overfishing of the oceans and accelerating climate changes. A lot of this is a function of the way that capitalism has essentially evolved throughout time. But this was not the original intention. Again, if we go back to Adam Smith, the Invisible Hand was oriented toward mutual benefit. Sadly, it's drifted far off track.

There is an argument that can be made that capitalism itself will encourage people to come up with solutions to create a greater good, meaning that the looming crisis with water and the environment will be addressed by figuring out better technologies to conserve and/or recycle water. This is certainly borne out when we look at the history of economic shifts caused by external shocks. These are what were largely responsible for the emergence of nascent capitalism following on the heels of feudalism 500 years ago.

Today, NASA, for example, has plans to develop a process to recycle human waste into food.[14] For the planned Mars expedition, astronauts will use technology to recycle human waste for water and energy—80 percent can be used again as food. Unappetizing as this may sound, the technology may actually translate into a viable solution to impending food shortages on this planet. It can be argued that although the dangers of running out of water or similar resources do exist, capitalism actually does begin to address and account for it. Does the argument work that left to its own devices (the profit motivation) industrial capitalism will just drive the creation of technologies to come up with the solution?

It could, but it's a huge gamble that it will indeed come up with a solution—the looming risk is that it will be far too late (as in the lily pad example). What's interesting is that historically it was external shocks that shaped the emergence of innovation. Let's consider a transition prior to the advent of the Industrial Age, where money in the form of credit began to emerge at the end of the feudal system. This was a key innovation. Credit was a nonstarter before the Industrial Age. The advent of trade required an innovation to sustain it.

We aren't saying that innovation isn't present today. It certainly is, but we think that the nature of "traditional" 20th-century capitalism is inhibiting that progress because it's focused on a concentration of wealth and the maintenance of a status quo born out of the existing paradigm.

As an example, today the ubiquity of information is eroding the market's ability to correctly form prices. That is because markets are based on scarcity while information is abundant. The system's defense mechanism is to entrench and form, essentially, monopolies—the giant tech companies, Monsanto with seed production, Big Pharma—on a scale not seen since the 1800s. We don't believe there is the time to wait for an organic adjustment to occur. Whenever we move into an era where hoarding becomes a focal point, transformative innovation begins to disappear.

A consciousness (and experience) of scarcity creates a fear-based physiology of contraction that squeezes innovation out of the existing system. Where innovation is beginning to appear as transformative alternatives to existing ways of doing business is in the emergence of shadow economies. These economies are disruptive alternatives that are unbound by the traditional constraints of modern-day capitalism.

Take Greece, for example. A shadow economy is emerging in the face of the extreme austerity requirements imposed on the Greeks by the EU and World Bank. Austerity strategies essentially squeeze out meaningful innovation, because everybody is required to retrench. It's a process of contraction that is oriented around a scarcity consciousness that says we have to maintain the status quo, or else we won't survive. Social unrest is the likely consequence of these types of austerity measures.

British journalist and broadcaster Paul Mason writes in an article entitled "The End of Capitalism Has Begun":

"Almost unnoticed, in the niches and hollows of the market system, whole swaths of economic life are beginning to move to a different rhythm. Parallel currencies, time banks, cooperatives and self-managed spaces have proliferated, barely noticed by the economics profession, and often as a direct result of the shattering of the old structures in the post-2008 crisis.

You only find this new economy if you look hard for it. In Greece, when a grassroots NGO mapped the country's food co-ops, alternative producers, parallel currencies and local exchange systems they found more than 70 substantive projects and hundreds of smaller initiatives ranging from squats to carpools to free kindergartens. To mainstream economics such things seem barely to qualify as economic activity— but that's the point. They exist because they trade, however haltingly and inefficiently, in the currency of postcapitalism: free time, networked activity and free stuff. It seems a meagre and unofficial and even dangerous thing from which to craft an entire alternative to a global system, but so did money and credit in the age of Edward III."[15]

We would like to see an alternative paradigm that can foster a sense of *thriving*, rather than just *surviving*. Compassionate capitalism provides such a possibility. All the austerity conversations revolve around survival of the existing capitalist-market framework. The resulting strategies are not oriented toward what can be done to restructure at-risk economies in a way that enables them to emerge into a sustainably healthier state. Choices made with thriving as the focal point are much different.

Yes, surviving is crucial—some of the at-risk economies require triage—but if the strategies employed don't include choices that will make possible long-term thriving—not just as a business, but also as a society and as a species—we doom ourselves. By considering choices that enable thriving as businesses and as a species, we have to take into account the rest of the ecosystem of which we're a part. If the rest of the ecosystem is dying, we won't survive, let alone thrive. There's an interconnectedness that needs to be accounted for and heeded. Which moves us into some of the reasons why a continued adherence to the existing capitalistic model is doomed.

We'll also add, since we are taking a worldview, not a local view, that the reality presented by differences among other existing economic models needs to be taken into account because the whole world is not capitalistic. Compassionate capitalism can be a model that also absorbs the models espoused by varied varieties of capitalism, communism, and socialism.

It will, we think, to a significant degree. There is little disagreement about this when examined in the light of evidence that the 200-year pattern of the industrial capitalist model is broken. Economic crisis has historically spurred new forms of technological innovation, which benefits everybody.

There are ways to begin this shift. One of them has to do with moving from speculation to true, long-term investment and not just the short-term speculative activities that today pass for investment in new technologies. Right now, our economic system rewards speculators. We have day traders who are in and out of a stock in nanoseconds, not because they're investing anything, rather they speculate (gamble) on market movements. This does not foster a longer-term healthy development of any new market sector, or new market initiatives, or market innovation.

An example of an alternative investment strategy that is aligned with the tenets of compassionate capitalism is that exemplified by Nobel Peace Prize winner and former U.S. Vice President Al Gore's Generation Investment Management firm. To quote from the November 2015 edition of *The Atlantic:* The firm serves "…as a demonstration of a new version of capitalism, one that will shift the incentives of financial and business operations to reduce the environmental, social, political, and long-term economic damage being caused by unsustainable commercial excesses. What this means in practical terms is that Gore and his Generation colleagues have done the theoretically impossible: Over the past decade, they have made more money, in the Darwinian competition of international finance, by applying an environmentally conscious model of 'sustainable' investing than have most fund managers who were guided by a straight-ahead pursuit of profit at any environmental or social price."

We can also look at some of the research data collected by the coauthor of *Conscious Capitalism,* Raj Sisodia, presented in his fascinating book *Firms of Endearment.*[16] The premise is, businesses that organize themselves explicitly around more altruistic values such as love, caring, and generosity are actually more successful than other businesses competing in the same market sectors. Some of the original firms surveyed include such well known names as BMW, Costco, Nordstrom, Starbucks, Panera Bread, Unilever, Tata, Ikea, Patagonia, Trader Joe's and Southwest Airlines. His data compared *Firms of Endearment* companies with the *Good to Great* companies touted by Jim Collins in his bestselling book by the same name. Both groups were compared against the S&P 500 Index for the period 1998-2013. The data suggest very convincingly that running a business with a set of values at its core other than profit or shareholder return is, in fact, good business.

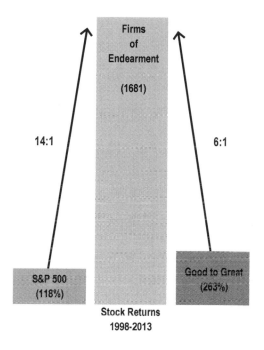

Firms
of
Endearment

(1681)

14:1

6:1

S&P 500
(118%)

Good to Great
(263%)

Stock Returns
1998-2013

(Source - *Firms of Endearment: How World-Class Companies Profit from Passion and Purpose* by Raj Sisodia, Jagdith Sheth, and David Wolfe. Adapted and used by permission from Raj Sisodia.)

Another way to facilitate a shift is to examine the notion of corporate immortality. There is nothing in nature that doesn't die, or at least doesn't face the prospect of death. While the American Revolutionary War was ostensibly fought against the rule of the British Crown, it was also waged against the monopoly of the British East India Company. The tea tossed into the Boston Harbor belonged to British East India Company, and it was destroyed in response to the British government passing the Tea Act of 1773. This tax allowed the Company to cheaply dump its tea in the Colonies in order to make a profit while also benefiting by taxing the tea. The monopoly enjoyed by the British East India Company was artificially extending the life of the Company past any useful value it was conferring on society as a whole.

Rather than being just an isolated incident that sparked a revolt, the problems caused by the artificial extension of life conferred by a monopoly was not overlooked by the emerging country born of that Revolution. Wary of the consequences of granting any charter that had no expiration date tied to the creation of useful value, it would be almost 100 years after winning its independence before America would again grant any kind of corporate charter. But it was only for public works projects such as railroads with the proviso that they could be revoked if the corporation caused significant harm.

Contrast this proviso against doing significant harm to the behavior of many of our largest companies today. In 2010, the U.S. Supreme Court in a 5-4 decision on the Citizens United case gave corporations the right given to spend money on political candidates of their choice as an expression of free speech. The consequence of this decision has been what can arguably be described as the selling of the political process to the organizations with the largest checkbook. In defense of the decision Cato Institute's Ilya Shapiro, who argued the case for Citizen's United, said, "Nobody is saying that corporations are living, breathing entities, *or that they have souls* or anything like that."[17]

If allowed to "die" a company can often be reborn in another incarnation. For an example of a company's natural "rebirth" into a new entity in service of evolving to changing needs as opposed to artificially extending the status quo, we need look no further than the Finnish telecommunications company Nokia. One of the authors of this book (Blaine) was a consultant to them for almost 12 years. The company was founded in 1865 as a pulp mill. Over the last 150-plus years it has reinvented itself over and over again. When Blaine started consulting with Nokia in the early 1990s, it still had a division that made and sold wire cable. It also sold rubber tires, rubber boots, farm implements, and television sets—plus, it had a small telephonic division.

With the collapse of the Soviet Union, Nokia (along with many of Finland's businesses) lost a significant percentage of its market. In response, it shifted its focus from being a regional conglomerate with a presence in a number of market sectors to that of a "player" in the emerging mobile telephony market. As a company, it took advantage of the expertise it had cultivated by being one of the developers (along with Sweden's Ericsson) of the Global System for Mobile (GSM) communications standard and parlayed it into ultimately becoming the largest supplier of mobile phones in the world by the end of the 1990s. The internal reinvention during this process of rebirth was significant and Blaine had the great opportunity to witness and influence it as he designed and delivered for 12 years a significant portion of their leadership development process.

Today Nokia is reinventing itself again. Like the fabled Phoenix, it faced impending "death" when the mobile phone market moved faster than it anticipated, only to rise again. Although its future is uncertain Nokia is continuing to do this with a focus on what value the market is needing that it can provide. And it's doing so without protectionist props.

The same pattern holds true in the National Football League (NFL). As evidence and publicity mounted concerning brain damage caused by repetitive concussions there is no doubt that the NFL has either delayed, denied or waited for the death of players before publicly acknowledging and beginning to address the tragic consequences to players subjected to the almost inevitable concussions they receive. The League is now confronting the problem that they helped to cause while recognizing that doing so has resulted in a great drop in the number of kids who actually participate in football. Not coincidentally, we're seeing a rise in the interest in other alternatives to football like flag football, lacrosse and soccer. This is not ideal for the NFL, but it is certainly progress born out of a different consciousness of awareness and accountability. Despite the risks to their bottom line they have finally decided to do what is surely the right (and compassionate) thing by making sure that people—especially children and their parents—are aware of the dangers of playing tackle football.

Ford Motor Company is also in the process of reinventing itself. It doesn't see itself as being in the auto manufacturing business anymore. It views itself as a business more in the broader sense of being a transportation company. It sees its future as not just a maker of vehicles, but as the foremost mobility company—one that prides itself on providing the best consumer experience. What it will provide doesn't just include wheels.

Ford sees a large part of their future customers in Millennials who don't want to buy cars today. Ride sharing has become a big part of their strategy. The question they considered is this: "How do we make available transportation modes for people who don't want to buy cars and see no need for a personal vehicle?" In 2016 at the North American International Auto Show, Ford unveiled a new app called FordPass. With it, Ford owners—or anyone else—will be able to use the app to get around more easily, thanks to car-sharing features and more. This is Ford Motor Company looking to the future rather than seeing itself expressed as an extension or modified version of the past. This is Ford shifting from the role of only manufacturing and selling vehicles to a brand new position: becoming the helpful, insightful brand that gets you where you want to go, whether it's behind the wheel of a Ford, on public transport, or ride sharing.

When organizations seek a broader perspective, when they explore how their services or products can begin to support and provide the opportunity for individuals to experience the joy in being alive as a consequence of their interacting with the business, then we have a whole new paradigm. The nature of "value" is being redefined in nonmonetary terms.

In this new economic model, it's not about how to get more money from each customer. Rather, it's about how the quality of life is impacted; bringing more satisfaction to the individual consumer's experience of living. If that possibility is present, consumers will not only want to buy a service or product, they will also feel good about doing so. Price in this model becomes essentially irrelevant to a significant degree. The advantage is to non-commoditize the product or service being offered by positioning it for a greater good, and simultaneously build a reputation as a compassionate corporation!

There is a quid pro quo that comes into play here, but it's driven by a different force: the notion of connection predicated on a consciousness of compassionate abundance that is different from what has traditionally been the case. It recognizes that humankind is not the overlord of nature. It's a force that is concerned with the up-leveling of the human experience, and the experience of living on the planet for the benefit of all life forms. Marc Benioff, chairman and CEO of Salesforce, said at the World Economic Forum in 2014, "The renowned economist Milton Friedman preached that the business of business is to engage in activities designed to increase profits. He was wrong. The business of business isn't just about creating profits for shareholders—it's also about improving the state of the world and driving *stakeholder* value."

In our modern society, the acquisition of money has become the default mechanism by which success is measured. That's where we think corporate greed has taken us seriously off the rails; and it's where one of the greatest opportunities exists for the compassionate organizations of tomorrow. The myopic and almost sociopathic focus on acquisition has brought us incredible wealth disparity, ill-considered deregulation that encouraged the financial services industries to morph into speculation, and thinly disguised gambling through the invention and use of exotic new financial instruments, such as derivatives, CDOs (collateralized debt obligations), and hedged CMO (collateralized mortgage obligation) tranches. Bankers and financiers call them investing mechanisms, but they're actually speculation mechanisms designed to give somebody the advantage to acquire more money quickly.

It's safe to say that in today's economic climate, the financial markets have lost their purpose and, consequently, the trust of the populace as a whole. The purpose of banking and finance used to be to develop funding sources to enable an organization to grow, to develop new technology, new services, new markets, and new products. But not any longer; their purpose has now become enabling investors (who are really speculators) so they can make money quicker. The 2015 Academy Award winning movie *The Big Short* provides an accurate and fascinating look into how this occurred.

The original idea behind establishing stock exchanges was to level the playing field so that anybody with interest and means could take part in developing promising markets and could potentially be rewarded for funding the incumbent risks of doing so. Exchanges were true investment vehicles. Today, the ability of institutions to take huge positions and market them via public relations and marketing to the masses in order to take advantage of the desire for quick returns is reflective of the speculative nature of the markets and of capitalism today. CEOs of Fortune 500 companies provide quarterly "guidance" in order to tell "investors" which way to "invest", knowing that the institutions that hold their stocks can usually manipulate the stock market to their advantage.

We also have elements of the financial industry that, through microsecond trading, can create waves of trading volume that artificially move the markets. This points to what the stock market has become— an arena for speculative investment versus investment for growth. That is the difference—and it is a difference that makes a difference. Speculative investment is largely behind the burgeoning growth of the Chinese economy today and, as a cautionary note to China, it was the sole source of the economic collapse of 2008.

The 2008 recession was caused by the failures of complex financial instruments created and managed by the world's largest hedge funds. By regulatory-design and extensive lobbying, these funds are not regulated. In addition to their huge presence in government lobbying circles[18] hedge funds have tremendous market power via the leverage provided by and through strategies employing exotic, thinly-traded instruments.

Some of the exotic strategies and instruments that were developed for the sole purpose of quick profit versus value investing, which can and are deployed and traded without regulatory scrutiny and oversight, are: event-driven, merger arbitrage, distressed securities, long-short, relative value, fixed-income, quantitative, convertible arb, mortgage-backed securities, tactical trading, discretionary and systematic, CDOs, CDS (credit-default swaps), and CMO tranches. The variety and sophistication boggles the mind and virtually no one understands them. It was estimated that there were $58 *trillion* CDS outstanding in 2007[19] that were NOT supported by tangible assets. These and more are legalized forms of gambling that were invented not as investment vehicles but as vehicles for insiders to speculate and reap huge profits.

Part of the reason for this is the changing nature of money itself. A point worth reiterating here is that it was a change in the nature of money (the invention of credit) that was one of the key catalysts for the movement from a feudal economy to the emerging capitalist economies of today. Currently, money is not the same as currency. Instead, money exists as bits of data in electronic accounts. It is seldom, if ever, actually touched, except in increasingly infrequent day-to-day transactions. If you recently bought a new car or any significant real estate, currency very likely did not change hands. The transaction was processed electronically using "virtual" currency.

Sub-Saharan Africa has been particularly innovative in harnessing technology for financial activities. The impact on the standard of living in the area has been dramatic. The region has experienced the fastest annual growth rates documented in the Human Development Index (HDI) advanced by the UN Development Program. The HDI is a summary measure of average achievement in key dimensions of human proficiency: a long and healthy life, being knowledgeable, and having a decent standard of living. It can be used to inform government policy decisions.

The emergence of M-Pesa, a mobile payment platform launched by Vodafone in Kenya in 2007, positioned that country as an innovation and technology hub in the region. Since its launch, M-Pesa has undergone explosive growth: In 2013, an incredible 43 percent of

Kenya's GDP[20] flowed through M-Pesa. With over 237 million person-to-person transactions[21] (in a country of 48 million people!) M-Pesa is universally present in the daily lives of Kenyans due to a range of services that include money deposit and withdrawal, remittance services, vendor payment, bill payment, and microcredit provision. All of this without any physical currency changing hands.

Also, look at BitCoin, an innovative payment network reputedly created by Satoshi Nakamoto in 2008. Here we have a virtual digital currency that you can invest, with no physical analog. It's all about bypassing the traditional financial ecosystem. Again, it's virtual. There is no tangible "product", nothing material that backs it. Yet it has proven to be impressively disruptive. BitCoin as a form of payment for products and services has grown, and merchants have an incentive to accept it because fees are lower than the 2–3% typically imposed by credit card processors. In fact, its legitimacy as a virtual currency can be seen in the fact that it has drawn the support of a few politicians, notably U.S. Senator Rand Paul, who accepts donations in BitCoin.

An interesting point of view to consider is the idea that money is imbued with a kind of immortality. People assume that money has no endpoint to its usefulness—we assume it doesn't expire. What would happen if money had an expiration date? What if some types of investments (particularly long-term, estate-sheltering strategies) had negative interest rates? You either use it or you lose it, so you have to keep it in circulation rather than hoarding it, which fosters true investment rather than speculation.

This isn't such a far-fetched idea any longer. A decade ago, the idea of negative interest rates was a theoretical curiosity. Beginning in 2014, negative interest rates began showing up as an unconventional step that a few small countries considered as a means of managing their economies and stimulating growth. Today, it is the stated policy of some of the most powerful global central banks, including the European Central Bank and the Bank of Japan.

On February 11, 2016, Sweden's central bank lowered its bank lending rate to a negative 0.5 percent from a negative 0.35 percent, and said it could cut further still; European bank stocks were hammered partly because investors feared what negative rates could do to bank profits. The Federal Reserve chairperson, Janet Yellen, acknowledged in congressional testimony that the American central bank was taking a look at the strategy.

This is a fascinating event to say the least. In 2015, Hervé Hannoun, then the deputy general manager of the Bank for International Settlements, argued that this could "over time encourage the use of alternative virtual currencies, undermining the foundations of the financial system as we know it today."

This is already beginning to occur. While BitCoin is likely the most well-known virtual currency, many more are making their appearance felt. Amongst Millennials, currency takes the form of game tokens that are every bit as "real" as traditional currency in as much as they can be used to purchase just about anything. Ethereum (ethereum.org) is a decentralized platform that, according to its website, "runs smart contracts: applications that run exactly as programmed without any possibility of downtime, censorship, fraud, or third party interference." It has the potential, according to William Quiqley, Managing Director at Clearstone Venture Partners of outpacing BitCoin as the dominant virtual currency in the world.

Is this "bad"? Today, we have financial services companies that provide no real (tangible) value to the economy. Their purpose is to support consumption, which contributes directly to our increasingly debt-fueled economy. As an example, one of the biggest and most successful of these companies is American Express, and it does nothing much except to charge fees to process transactions.

Rampant consumerism (or consumption) is the basis for debt-fueled economic growth. In order to continue growing the world economy, there's research to suggest that we will need to take on more debt in the next 15 years than there is money in the world to support it. The World Economic Forum says that global credit will need to double to $210 trillion by 2020 in order to provide the necessary credit-driven growth for world GDP to *retain* its current growth rate. As of this writing every single person and country in the world is estimated to "owe" a grand total of $199 trillion, with some 29% of it borrowed since the 2008 financial crisis.[22] Contrast this to the amount of available money. M_3 is a measure of the amount of money that includes physical money, savings and checking accounts, CDs, institutional money market funds, long term deposits and other convertible assets. It is estimated to be approximately $75 trillion. Was this trend also true 15 years ago? Yes, it was true then, but nobody crunched the numbers in quite this way. How does our recent recovery affect this opinion? Not by much if at all. The underlying dynamics of growth dependent on debt remains in place.

Again, consider the examples of Haiti, Greece, and Spain. They were forced to take on huge debts to build their economies, and now they can't repay them. The International Money Fund (IMF) and the World Bank go crazy, and the economy begins to tumble. There's no good reason outside of an interlocking, economic, banking structure invested in continually rising debt, that a nation state can't go its own way. And when the institutional lenders force a country into austerity measures, the nation often ends up no better off than if it had never taken the loans in the first place.

For an increasing number of people, virtual currencies represent a way to move beyond continuing to support and be part of what many see as an irreparably broken financial system. As impactful as the emergence of credit was to the growth of pre-industrial capitalism, so too may be the impact of these new currencies in disrupting and changing post-industrial capitalism. Organizing these new financial activities around the ideals espoused by a compassionate capitalism model will create emerging opportunities for astute businesses that are paying attention.

CHAPTER 3

The Changing Nature of Value Creation

"A human being is part of a whole, called by us the Universe, a part limited in time and space. He experiences himself, his thoughts and feelings, as something separated from the rest – a kind of optical delusion of his consciousness. This delusion is a kind of prison for us, restricting us to our personal desires and to affection for a few persons nearest us. Our task must be to free ourselves from this prison by widening our circles of compassion to embrace all living creatures and the whole of nature in its beauty."
~ Albert Einstein

As mentioned earlier, every story has psychology, physiology, and philosophy associated with it. And as we ponder our possible economic futures, all these dimensions will continue to be in play.

The *psychology* of the capitalism story (which deals with cause and effect) is changing. This is in large part a function of access to information, the speed by which we gather it, and the breadth of what is available. The lag in information distribution is decreasing dramatically and business needs are a key driver. Clearly, business is the most pervasive and influential force on the planet; and as a consequence, has both a moral and a functional responsibility for the effects that are being caused by its activities.

In terms of the *physiology* of the story, the industrial-capitalist model was born of a feudal legacy exemplified by a lord-serf relationship that is mirrored in modern boss-worker roles. Today we see that the buying and selling of labor (as evidenced within the boss-worker roles) is being replaced by a model that is changing traditional reporting structures and is based on paying for contribution. From a physiological standpoint, this changes the shape of how business is conducted.

Historically, the industrial economic model was based on a sense of obligation as evidenced with the lord-serf relationship. It was assumed that if you gave me a job, I would feel obligated to give you my labor and that you would own the fruits of my labor. This is in contrast to an increasingly more common arrangement today (particularly with the Millennial generations), where work (and my work product) is more and more seen as a valued extension of my life. The net is that the "boss" or the organization does not by default "own" my time or my work product. One consequence of this is that retirement becomes less enticing as something to look forward to . . . so much so that it's possible that we can envision a point in time where the idea of retirement becomes obsolete.

We can both cite personal examples where this is becoming more commonplace. Blaine had a conversation recently with an old friend on a flight from Tampa to Seattle. Carol's 70th birthday was two weeks away, and she was excited about starting a new business at a time when most people traditionally look toward retirement. She is a well-respected psychologist with a thriving practice and was looking forward to "what's next?" Not because anything was broken, but because she wanted more from her life and was truly eager to see how that would be expressed in her future.

We're shifting from the American Association of Retired Persons (AARP) to what Brian Smith (founder of UGG boots) now calls Boomerpreneur. UGG is from Australia, so "Boomer" not only means Baby Boomer, but also describes a BIG wave with an incredible amount of energy. Brian sees the same thing in creating a multimillion-dollar organization with Boomerpreneurs as part of their employee base. These Boomerpreneurs can shift our belief that there's an end to when we personally provide value in our society to actually having continual "rebirths" at 50, 60, 70, 80, even 90 years of age.

We recently met the founder of the world-renowned Rancho La Puerta Spa in Tecate, Mexico. At the age of 93, Deborah Szekely told us, "I'm doing the third rendition of my website. I started my first website at 91." That's the Boomerpreneur. This is a significant shift away from the industrial capitalist worker's aspiration of, "I will retire when I'm 65 and never have to work again." This notion of retiring from work is fueled by the experience of being a cog in a large wheel whereby one's individual labor is essentially indistinguishable from that of others. Again, this represents a change in the physiology of the capitalist story . . . physically, it is no longer a viable reality because people are now living to 100 or beyond, and that's just from our generation. Millennials can expect to have that age become the expected norm. Furthermore, just the idea of stopping work will be something that's almost an embarrassment—an indication that we're not physically capable of providing value.

The employment contracts we saw back in the 1940s–50s were predicated in part on shorter lifespans. Today, as people live longer and have access to more recreational, social, and life-affirming choices, the need to retire begins to disappear. Again, we go back to what's meaningful in people's lives. Carol's eyes lit up when she spoke about this new project she was taking on. That's not something that our parents or grandparents necessarily evidenced. The physiology of the capitalist story is a big marker to pay attention to, as it is beginning to inform the emergence of a new way of doing business.

Additionally, we can look to the field of neurobiology to understand the physiological impact of compassion. In the human body, meditating and focusing on compassion and acts of kindness engendered in part by empathy results in a direct impact on the vagus nerve. This is a bundle of nerves that originate in the top of the spinal cord and directly controls the body's parasympathetic nervous system, which is in control of the relaxation response. The vagus nerve functions to activate and regulate different organs throughout the body such as the heart, lungs, liver, and digestive organs. The stimulation and activation of this nerve has a direct correlation on improved heart health, reduction in stress hormones, increases in oxytocin (the neurotransmitter most directly related to bonding, trust, and connecting with others). Research also suggests that that activation of the vagus nerve is associated with development of the ethical intuition that humans from different social groups (even adversarial ones) are fundamentally connected. People who have high vagus nerve activation in a resting state are prone to feeling emotions that promote altruism—compassion, gratitude, love, and happiness. Recognition of this fact is so intriguing that it is generating a fascinating research focus about the nature of altruism itself: Is there a branch of our nervous system that evolved to support such behavior?

If we extrapolate from the human phenomenon to the phenomenon of capitalism and business, what analogs might we find? While the metaphor of money as the "blood" of the economic system is certainly apt, it may be useful to explore what serves as the vagus nerve of the capitalism body. Similar to how the body's vagus nerve coordinates with the parasympathetic system to control the heart and digestive functions, what might influence how money flows through the body of the economy and affect the nature of how we consume resources? One thought is the discarded and neglected "Invisible Hand" espoused by Adam Smith. Similar to the real vagus nerve it could be a core "nerve" that regulates many, if not all, capitalist functions. Under-activated, one would expect to see blockages in the flow of money, increased stress in the economic body, over-consumption, and an absence of connection. What would be the impact on the story that is capitalism if the Invisible Hand was activated with a focus on compassion and with acts of kindness engendered by empathy? Such an approach would certainly be the antithesis of how the activity of business is generally held in today's economic model and could have a dramatic impact on how the narrative of a new capitalism unfolds.

We think that the *philosophy* of the industrial capitalist story is also changing. Philosophy speaks to why we do as we do. More and more, there's a realization that we're all in this together. We're reminded of a cartoon that shows two guys in the front of a boat, and two guys in the back where there's a hole and water is gushing in. The guys in the back are bailing water as fast as they can, while the guys in the front are merely looking at them. One front man says to the other, "I'm sure glad the hole isn't in our end. . ." We are ALL in the same boat. This is becoming more evident when we start looking at conversations about the health of the environment and about wealth sharing.

How we define value is being increasingly questioned. It's not just shareholder value any longer. It's not just monetary return on an investment that is considered to be value.

We believe there are three converging dynamics feeding into this new value story: Digitization, collaboration, and abundance consciousness. They're all the consequences of the availability of information. We have access to information now in ways that we've never had it historically. There are some interesting things that come as a consequence of that, digitization being probably the most dramatic. We think that digitization will be the most disruptive market force of the 21st century. Digitization results in commoditization of products and services because it increases access exponentially and it decreases the price point of goods and services; the cost of production almost disappears. We see this evidenced in pharmaceuticals, music, publishing, transportation, construction, entertainment, manufacturing, medicine, literally every market sector.

The rapid increase and access to information is corroding the market's ability to form prices correctly. Markets historically were based on scarcity, and information scarcity is no exception. When information is abundant, scarcity becomes a nonissue and cost is correspondingly negligible. Again, this speaks to the impact of digitization.

A great example of the disruptive impact of ubiquitous information access is 3D printing: We're now printing tools on the International Space Station that mitigate the need to ship parts to space. For the first time a pharmaceutical pill was recently digitally printed. There are plans to 3D print a skyscraper. A car has already been "printed". Organs are being "printed" for transplantation. General Electric recently used a technique known as Direct Laser Metal Melting (DLMM) for printing the first 3D-printed part to be certified by the American FAA—a fuel nozzle—for installation in its GE90 jet engine. DLMM works by laying down a fine metallic powder in a flat layer, then a laser fuses a section of the engine's CAD plan within it. Another layer of dust is laid down and the process is repeated. When the printing is completed, the excess powder is blown and brushed away, and the part is given a finish. The result is a product that is both 25% lighter in weight, as well as a staggering five times more durable than its older sibling, all of which translates to a savings of around $3 million per aircraft, per year for any airline flying a plane equipped with the engine This is extremely disruptive and the potential for what this makes possible in terms of access to free time, access to creativity, and access to a lot of different things that go into defining value begins to suggest that how we define "value" is open to radical/revolutionary redefinition.

The convergence and availability of information also begins to redefine how we view the collaborative production and delivery of goods and services in organizations. As we write this, Uber has a market valuation of $63 billion, and it has only been in operation for about three years. AirBnB isn't far behind. Lyft is in that same category. These organizations don't respond to the dictates of a traditional market force and they obviate traditional management and labor hierarchies. There's a lot of dynamics in play that are beginning to force a change in the way that we think about capitalism and the creation of value itself.

As can be expected in the face of any revolution, there is pushback from the existing established players. The legal side of this is emerging as the primary battleground. For example, in many US states, legislation is being pushed to prohibit Uber from competing with the medallion taxi services. The issue is that to maintain a traditionally competitive landscape, licensing, training, and certification are necessary. The context supporting this is that Uber drivers must be treated as traditional labor and it is positioned under the pretense of safety. The effect is essentially the process of traditional stakeholders trying to force scarcity on consumers when someone comes up with a completely abundant and ubiquitous way to share rides and make it economical and profitable.

Recently, when Blaine was in Seattle, he met a young man who claimed that driving for Uber has changed his life; he makes twice as much money as before. He was a commercial window washer and he now also has three times as much time to spend with his seven-month-old daughter. Blaine had another conversation with an Uber driver in Tampa about his ability to pick up people at the airport (many Uber drivers are forbidden by local ordinance from serving airports).

Blaine asked, "Where's the pushback?"

The man explained that it's not from the taxi drivers, because Florida taxi drivers are not organized. Instead, the opposition is coming from the attorneys. To paraphrase what the driver essentially said, "The lawyers have their fingers in a lot of pies that are commingled with licensing. Where cab drivers drop people off, there are rebates that come back, so when you start following the money, it gets interesting."

With proposed legislation to classify Uber drivers as employees, rather than independent contractors, the government is trying to maintain the scarcity model instead of allowing these futuristic, accelerated, abundant, value-driven companies to prosper.

This is where we will witness the clash, and it is where we pay attention to see how this plays out. Interestingly, a paradigm that has the capacity to absorb a competing paradigm, will be the one that dominates. A scarcity paradigm cannot hold up to an abundance paradigm. Scarcity does not have the capacity to absorb abundance. However, abundance does have the capacity to account for scarcity, so it will eventually subsume and overtake it as the dominant paradigm. That's a direct consequence of access to information. One only need look at what occurred in the recording industry when Napster appeared on the scene in 1999. Napster was a peer-to-peer network that enabled 80 million registered users to freely and easily share music with each other. It was sued by the major labels, the Recording Industry of America, and a number of mainstream musicians for copyright infringement and forced into bankruptcy. But the genie was out of the bottle. The recording artist Dave Mathews (Dave Mathews Band) said, "Napster: It is the future, in my opinion. That's the way music is going to be communicated around the world. The most important thing now is to embrace it." Today, the recording landscape is dramatically different as a consequence of a larger and more abundant paradigm.

The abundance model will shine a light on what a consciousness of scarcity artificially created. This is directly related to how we define value and how value is created. In the future, value will be less defined by monetary return driven by scarcity of access. It will remain a major part of the equation, but less so over time. In the future, the longtime model of "supply and demand" will be an increasingly irrelevant factor in how commerce is conducted. Business will no longer be able to use artificial supply constraints to drive up or maintain high prices solely for the purpose of creating profit.

Back in the 1930s, John Maynard Keynes said that at some point the economic ideal envisioned with capitalism takes hold and actually works. Humankind's real problem will become "how to use his freedom from pressing economic cares . . . to live wisely and agreeably and well."[23] The implications for the capitalistic economic model are significant. An artifact of the economic model that post-industrial capitalism doesn't speak to, and Keynes didn't speak to, is how do we work more when economic necessity is not driving us to do so?

Part of the inefficiency in the industrial capitalism model is the ability of one agent to broker the services of another while controlling the access to information and ubiquity that it provides. Whether it's real estate, jets, cab rides, manufacturing, or purchasing, there's no need for a middle person. You can go directly to the manufacturer or provider or, as is the case with 3D printing, not even need a manufacturer or provider. There are no middle people involved. It's almost direct access from idea to material goods or services. The elimination of inefficiencies creates such time savings and value for everyone involved that we can create, with the shift in the paradigm, more value, more abundance, and, if we are careful, we can create and continue to get closer to a utopian society.

That's where the conversation about compassion is relevant. Philosopher Arthur Schopenhauer said that "compassion is the basis of morality." As a thesis for this book, we're basically taking the position that compassion is the prerequisite to both responsibility and consciousness. Compassion is the behavior warranted by increasing consciousness. It is imperative if we are to create a socially just and morally wealthy society. This becomes important when we observe how things get done. When we look at the increasing transparency that results from access to information, companies can't hide how they conduct business anymore. Compassion almost becomes a prerequisite to making mindful, intelligent decisions and choices about the welfare of all concerned—of all stakeholders.

Compassion is an interesting word. It's derived from the ancient Greek word *pashko,* which literally translates to passion. Passion has a couple of definitions that are worth examining. On the one hand, passion means to care so much about something that one is willing "to suffer" for its realization—as in the passion of Christ. Literally, what is it that we have decided is meaningfully worth "suffering" for? Interestingly, suffering does not require pain. Another definition of passion is to feel keenly or to experience fully. Pain is not required yet the vulnerability of being open to feeling keenly or experiencing fully can, for many, be painful. It's at this nexus of keen feeling and profound meaning that we are most alive and most connected to our world. When we put this in the context of capitalism, it's the positioning of an organization, an entire economy, to feel keenly, to experience fully what it means to be alive and connected; what it means to be both creating and delivering, plus receiving value that is life affirming. That reciprocity becomes part of the defining factor of economic activity. It's not about scarcity, but about passionate access to the ability to experience fully what it means to be human, to be connected to life. This probably sounds abstract and utopian, but there's a fundamental business case to be made here, which we will explore in the next chapter.

In 1894, William H. Lever introduced the Royal Disinfectant Soap to the U.K. as an agent that would be effective in combating germs and still be affordable to the masses. In 1895, it was rebranded as Lifebuoy and marketed as a personal hygiene product by Lever Brothers (a predecessor to Unilever). Lifebuoy became one of the top selling soaps in North America through the middle of the last century. Today, the brand promise of Unilever is to change the hygiene behavior of a billion consumers across Asia, Africa, and Latin America. Their advertising promotes the benefits of hand washing at key occasions during the day, thereby reducing respiratory infections and diarrheal diseases, the world's two biggest causes of child mortality. Unilever has taken on the challenge to change the way that a billion people on this planet have access to rudimentary hygiene tools such as Lifebuoy—a product that is over 100 years old, in order to reduce the consequence of some of the most devastating diseases for kids. This is altruism expressed in a business context.

In India (the country with the highest number of children under five dying from diarrheal diseases), if hand washing is increased by one time a week, those deaths are reduced by about 400 per day.[24] It's a phenomenal statistic. Of course, Unilever links the Lifebuoy brand to some of its marketing and sales efforts, but altruism still is a key part of the dynamic. Unilever is looking at the contribution to a greater whole— taking an existing legacy product that is more than 100 years old and saying that as a consequence of some of the ways that they go to market,

"We can make a difference in how life is experienced on this planet. We can enable people to experience fully what it means to be alive and connected." This, we think, is a good example of what compassionate capitalism can be. If we activate the vagus nerve of the Invisible Hand by simply combining compassion with capitalism, we end up with a way to transform how we live and experience life as we know it on this planet. We create value of a very different sort.

This goes back to business being the most pervasive force on the planet today. We believe business leaders (and we use the term leader in the way it was defined in the Introduction—everyone is a leader) have a moral responsibility to affect a transformation in how life is lived on the planet, by taking into account the impact of the actions of business regarding all life.

CHAPTER 4

The Creation of Value: The Role of Soul

"Every time we've made a decision to do the right thing,
it ends up being good business."
~ Yvon Chouinard, Founder of Patagonia

Dave ran the largest sports agency in the world, in one of the scarcest businesses in the world: sports talent. His story is informative:

"The scarcity is created by the limited number of professional athletes who are available, hence a finite resource to monetize. It was in this environment that I experienced an individual I consider to be a true compassionate leader. Leigh Steinberg is a humanitarian and altruistic individual. I was fascinated by how he could be so fundamentally unmotivated by the money that was such an integral part of our business. He was more concerned about creating a legacy for his clients by requiring every client to create a foundation to give back to his or her community. His clients have donated over $600 million to charities around the world.[25] In this he was truly a pioneer. It wasn't easy for him or us and it took a toll. Ultimately, Hall of Fame quarterback Warren Moon and I left the company and started our own firm to carry on Leigh's legacy of giving back. What we set out to build was this compassionate company—a business with a soul.-

Moving forward, we looked at this scarce vertical and asked ourselves, 'How can we shift the paradigm? What are the key components of what we're trying to do within this emotional business?' We looked at three key components. We felt that creating abundance [making a lot of money] in order to help a lot of people, while having a lot of fun would be how we'd define whether or not we were successful [note the psychology, philosophy, and physiology of this approach]. It was our position that if we ran a company that focused on those three things, we could change what people believe this business is about.

Everything we do surrounds itself with the right people and the right ideas. We bring the celebrities, athletes, entertainers, media, high-net wealth individuals to projects that aligns them with the biggest sporting and entertainment events in the world. The Super Bowl, pro golf, the Masters, the Kentucky Derby and Breeder's Cup, ESPYs, Emmys, Oscars, right back to the Newport Beach and Sundance Film Festivals.

We believed that while creating value or abundance, we also needed to include a fourth key component (which is now a third of our business) that is oriented around giving back. So everything that we do must have an altruistic or a charitable component to it. If the business model doesn't have all of these components, we move to the next thing. That's what happened externally. What happened internally was that we wanted (as our personal and professional mission) to empower others to empower still others.

The idea was that if we could teach 100 employees how to do something, that would be great. But what if we could empower each of these people to empower another 100, or more? We wanted to nurture the nurturers. Not just in order for them to be abundant, and to shift the paradigm of this value, but (more importantly) to train them to train others. And if each of those 100 could train 100, to train 100, to train 100, we could create a collective belief.

That collective belief would be that this industry, which is one of the most successful industries in America (as measured in "traditional" terms), could be seen as an abundant value creator instead of a scarce, competitive, even backstabbing type of industry. That scarcity consciousness exists from top to bottom in the industry, whether it's ownership of teams, to networks, all the way to internships. We decided, from top to bottom, to build our business in a manner that reflected our belief that the world, indeed the universe, is abundant. It was an intentional and mindful educational process . . . and today we have more interns than we have employees.

In the short term, from an economic standpoint, this model might not benefit our business; but in the long term, we know it will not only benefit Sports 1 Marketing, but society as a whole by empowering and showing these young minds exactly how they can exponentially create value without taking value."

If we view this as a journey to the soul of business, part of our conversation is steeped in the notion that this *soul* is rooted in the truth that all things are connected.

Let's stop for a moment and consider how we define *soul*. In Aristotelian philosophy, the soul is considered the animating or vital force inherent in all living things. It's what endows them to various degrees with the potential to grow and reproduce, move and respond, to think rationally and behave compassionately, which is rooted, again, in the notion of everything being connected in some way.

Fundamentally, all human beings seek (even if only subconsciously) to enhance their experience of being fully and joyfully alive in their skin. I want to feel more alive day to day. I want to feel uplifted. I want to feel there's this possibility of joy that wouldn't be accessed if I were not in my skin today. Thus, value creation for my business can be defined as bringing the possibility of having access to uplifting experiences of living to all who come in contact with my product or my service. But not just the individual humans we come into contact with, rather expanding this into including the experience that all life in the ecosystem will have. This speaks to how we consume, dispose, and honor resources in the production of our products or services.

We love the way that Sports 1 Marketing identified that as part of the inherent context it operates within. In the sports arena, there are a finite number of pro athletes, as an example, so how do you move away from a consciousness of scarcity as the defining element of value in this competitive space and shift the paradigm of value into something that's a bit more altruistic?

Sports 1 Marketing has what can be called an "inspired business". There is an emotional and spiritual connection regardless of your belief, be it in God, Jesus, Buddha, Muhammad, Shiva, Joseph Smith, Spirit, Consciousness, or source/energy. Their purposeful, inspired business is what makes people want to create (and not just *take*) value.

They've expanded this into other areas as well. An example is a project they call Processing for a Cause. Sports 1 is working with First Data, the world's largest merchant service company who, instead of paying celebrities and athletes to endorse their services, encourages them to shift the paradigm and visit companies Sports 1 solicits and ask them to switch over to First Data. If they do, a portion of the bank fees that they already pay will go to the charity of their choice. This is an annuity, it will continue to go to the charity seamlessly and effortlessly. The program is based on continuing to do what you do today and in the process give back to your organization by supporting an aligned charity.

We see this program as a classic example of how abundance can be created for everyone within the perspective of compassionate capitalism. The program helps create an abundant environment...one in which everyone wins.

It's a unique business model where you take the epitome of inspiration—sports, and our sports heroes—and market their "stories". Many of us are inspired by the feats of these famous athletes—we "feel" more alive as a consequence of hearing their stories. How to parallel the business side of sports into the same type of inspiration is what Sports 1 is doing.

Inspired living. The etymology of inspire is rooted in aspiration, which has to do with breathing. So what am I breathing as a business? What am I breathing into my business? What is breathing my business? Aspirations, inspiration, all these things come into play when we look at the nature of the soul of business, and the creation of value in this process.

Most pundits and business writers use the Apple company as an example in some form. I (Blaine) recall purchasing my first iPhone and (this goes back to how we define value) feeling thrilled to be alive as a consequence of having access to this unique product. What was fascinating to me, was that I was ecstatic about the box that this instrument came in—the packaging. I still have it! I hadn't even unwrapped it yet to get to the phone, and I was mesmerized by the packaging. There was something about the way that this box's design held the promise of the product that I said I wanted, which was the iPhone. This was a bespoke design that took the end user's *experience* into account. I know from conversations with people that knew him well that Steve Jobs oriented the entire design process as it moved from the beginning of ideation, all the way through the delivery process so that *my* experience was always the focus.

The manufacturing, production, and delivery process to the end user experience, was the key determinant to every decision that was made about the packaging, the phone's design, even how it gets unwrapped when opened. None of these things were accidental. When we look at inspiration, when we consider the creation of value, we view it through the lens of, "How can I do this in a way that is intended to delight, to bring the experience of 'Wow! I am so glad I'm alive today,' as I hold this product and/or as I have access to this service?"

That's compassion writ large, and I will pay a premium for that kind of value. It's not coincidental that, as of this writing, Apple is the most valued company, based on market cap, on the planet today. It's a consequence of that kind of focus. Does it get everything right? Absolutely not! But more often than not, Apple pays attention to and delivers on the right things.

And this revolves around the notion of value, and it's not *shareholder* value that we're referring to. That's not the way that Apple determines the quality of its business, it's not the way it determines which products come next to market. When Apple's CEO Tim Cook was chided for Apple's investments in curbing climate impact, his response spoke directly to this notion. "When we work on making our devices accessible by the blind, I don't consider the bloody ROI," Cook said, adding that the same sentiment applied to environmental, health and safety issues. He told Justin Danhof of the National Center for Public Policy Research, an active lobbyist against action to tackle climate change, that if he did not believe in climate change, he should sell his Apple shares. "If you want me to do things only for ROI reasons, you should get out of this stock," Cook said.[26] The litmus test is the impact on the quality of life. "Does this delight? Does this bring the opportunity to experience 'God, I love that I'm alive today!'?"

David has an example of the role of love and value creation, using an example of a pen.

"This is the personal shift that took place from someone who came from a sales background where I could oversell, back-end sell, and take value. The objective of my capitalistic training in business was to take from the client value that was greater than the value I was giving. This system was based on a matter of manipulation and scarcity. Sales, like I said, includes (for most) overselling, back-end selling, and emotional attachment. Where this system always falls short is, if we are taking more than we're giving in any socioeconomic structure, you're actually creating a void, a shortage, an obstacle, and resistance, which then creates a feeling of scarcity.

When you create a void there's not enough of something. So if I have twenty dollars, but I can persuade someone to give me a hundred dollars of value for my twenty dollars, it might seem like the deal of a lifetime. But it's actually not good in the end, because it creates a perpetual cycle of manufactured shortages, obstacles, and resistance, or scarcity. It reinforces a zero sum process of one-upmanship, with somebody always feeling they got the short end of the stick.

But if you *provide* value that's equal to or greater than what you're asking for, it creates the opposite. It creates abundance, and the value itself will fill up to what you are providing. Look to the example of Steve Jobs, and why he was so successful— Apple now generates five percent of the US gross national product (GNP). That experiential value is greater than the $800 that we pay today for the iPhone.

I utilize what I call the pen value example to illustrate this point. I can take any pen, a regular plastic Bic pen, and sell it to anyone for a million dollars. Here's how: I could give you a million-dollar loan at no interest, and I would guarantee that at the end of one year, if you couldn't resell that plastic pen for two million dollars, I'd relieve you of your debt. I'd also place in escrow, with a person of your choice, a million dollars that I'd remit in an instant back to you if you hadn't sold the pen.

Of course, anyone and everyone would take that business opportunity because it gives more value than it receives, regardless of the value of the inanimate object, or what you're actually giving. In my new perspective the value has to be greater than that which you're asking."

Indeed, value is becoming increasingly less defined by scarcity. In fact, it's becoming more dependent on the *lack* of scarcity, and how that ends up becoming defined. As we've seen, digitalization today is disrupting markets in a fundamental way. When something becomes digitized, production costs decline to near zero, and we are left only with the question of distribution.

Because information is increasingly abundant and available, scarcity as a consequence becomes less relevant as a market mechanism that is central to setting price. When something gets digitized, essentially what's been created is access to information. Again, 3D printing is probably one of the greatest examples of this. You will start seeing advancements in the medical field where this is going to become another amazing solution in terms of how drugs are delivered.

Digitization will be one of the most interesting value plays when we consider how pharmaceuticals are produced, moving us into a Star Trek type era. The role of value here will become more and more defined by the players who are willing to explore and embrace innovative and disruptive technologies. Blaine is involved with a late stage startup company that is using emerging quantum technology that bypasses completely traditional pharmaceutical treatments for late stage cancers. Because there is no manufacturing what is the cost basis? This is where new metrics come into play, so rather than having a single bottom line, we measure not only profit, but also the impact on people, on places, and on the planet.

JUST Capital is an independent nonprofit information platform that seeks to measure and track corporate performance based on the American public's definition of just business behavior. Each year, they survey more than 40,000 Americans to find out what they believe defines corporate justness. From there, they measure how corporations are performing, based on the values of the American public, then release an annual report ranking the most Just companies.

All of this speaks to a redefinition of value, and it becomes amenable to triple (or even quadruple) bottom-line accounting. It begins to enable a move from scarcity, which is oriented around concepts of surviving, to more of a generative process, which is fundamentally steeped in the assumption of abundance and allows us to thrive. One of the things that we've always had some difficulty with is the business aphorism, "It's a jungle out there, and only the strong survive."

There are two difficulties we have with that assertion. One is that "only the strong survive" is not the point that Darwin was making. He actually meant that those who can cooperate and adapt the best will end up being the most dominant.[27] The second difficulty is with the implication that a jungle is a hostile or dangerous place to be. If that were true, then a desert would be more preferable. Unfortunately, a desert doesn't present a lot of opportunity for thriving. Within a jungle, there is a lushness, there is abundance, there is a lot of variety, diversity, and there is a lot of opportunity. We would, quite frankly, rather be in a jungle than in a desert.

Navigating well in a lush jungle becomes an interesting opportunity, an interesting concept to play with. That is where thriving comes into play. When you think of a thriving garden, it's abundant, it's lush, diversity abounds, and it creeps out of its boundaries. There's enough resources to go around. The consciousness of abundance is key to this shift – abundance in resources as well as abundance generated by cooperation.

The economic benefits become geometric in the way that they unfold. Blaine often travels to Africa and India as part of his role on the board of the Unstoppable Foundation.[28] One of his colleagues in Africa mentioned something he calls an economic merry-go-round, and Blaine got curious. They were talking about economic development, and Blaine mistakenly thought that they were talking about something in the nature of micro-lending, but it wasn't that at all.

Essentially what they were discussing was a process for creating economic development opportunity. Beginning with tribal women in particular, the first step in the process was to vet them for their willingness to "play by the rules". Part of that had to do with their attitude. Were they willing to come to an economic development opportunity with the understanding that everybody is not only in this together, but they are also in this for the long haul? Once they got a vetted cohort of women assembled, each woman put a certain amount of money into a sort of escrow account.

It was a nominal amount. These tribal members live on less than two dollars a day, so we're talking abject poverty. But they'd find enough money to put into this account every month, and once a month, one of the women had access to all the funds, for whatever project she wanted to invest in. It could be community beehives, buying a new goat for the herd, or buying a brick-making machine to enable the construction of a new home for her family. It was her choice and it could be anything that was practical.

The merry-go-round provided a resource that moved people, from a consciousness standpoint, out of the notion of scarcity and into the idea of abundance. There's now an abundant resource of money for one of the members of the merry-go-round to have access to something they can leverage to be creative and innovative.

The success of this has been phenomenal. There's nothing to pay back. It's all about contributing, and it's treating money not as a currency of exchange or barter but as energy. Money is energy, and when money gets stopped, like water held back by a dam, there's little utility to that. As long as the money is flowing, and flowing in an effective manner, you can manifest a lot of things.

In those areas in Africa and India where the Unstoppable Foundation is doing developmental work, we have women who lift their families (and eventually their villages) out of poverty. They buy a goat and create a milk business. They buy a sewing machine and create a tailor business. They buy a refrigeration unit and provide a dairy co-op. This is in an area where just about everyone is living at a subsistence level. Yes, it's good to feed and house your family, but you'll never get ahead without a change of paradigm—from scarcity to abundance.

It's fascinating to watch these women. They laugh, they dance, and they sing. They are vibrantly alive, and it's a function, in part, of the economic model that they're actually participating with. All of a "sudden", they now have a milk co-op where they've never had even the ability to store milk before. It's taken a couple of years, but they now have a refrigeration facility where they can store the milk—providing more choices to the women for how they feed their families and having the experience of feeling more joyfully alive. It is a result of the new way they approach opportunity, and it's how they define value. Providing economic relief from crushing poverty is one thing and it's necessary. Changing a poverty of mind is far more sustainable.

In October 2015, the U.S. Securities and Exchange Commission (SEC) voted on and passed rules to implement Title III of the JOBS Act—giving non-accredited investors the right to invest in companies via crowdfunding. As a consequence of the ruling, companies can now offer and sell securities through crowdfunding platforms, such as Crowdfunder.com and Angel.com. This ruling could unleash trillions of investment dollars now locked up in personal savings, IRAs, and investment accounts that sit around and basically only finance large companies in the public market. This capital will go on to fuel thousands of bold entrepreneurs who want to tackle the world's most difficult problems or take the biggest moonshots. By aligning incentives, early investors will be able to participate in the upside of successful companies that are redefining value.

It's a shifting of a myopic focus of *me* to *we*. Moving from being the best *in* the world, to being the best *for* the world. Moving from "What's in it for me?" to "What's the highest good?" Those sort of things all come into play here, and it is a shift not in value and the way we're defining it here, but a shift in *values*, what we pay attention to. This is where the soul of business begins to make a difference.

Referring again to the Aristotelian definition of soul, it's the animating or vital principle that endows us with the potential to grow, and to move and respond, to think rationally, to feel connected, and to feel valued. That's what we want to see as being possible with compassionate capitalism. It is a journey to that soul, via a redefinition of what it means to create value, and what value truly is in the business process. Period.

CHAPTER 5

Authenticity and the Compassionate Capitalist

And the deepest level of communication is not communication, but communion. It is wordless. It is beyond words, and it is beyond speech, and it is beyond concept. Not that we discover a new unity. We discover an older unity. My dear brothers, we are already one. But we imagine that we are not. And what we have to recover is our original unity. What we have to be is what we are.

~ Thomas Merton

A s defined earlier, a leader is anybody who causes movement in a system. That's the simplest definition we can think of. This description is free of behavioral characteristics and free of personality. It speaks to the fundamental question of *what does a leader actually do?* At the end of the day, because they cause movement he or she also causes things to be different.

The question that we're exploring here is partly, how does a compassionate capitalist working within a compassionately capitalistic organization function as a leader? That question moves into a conversation about the nature of effective leadership. We define leadership as the activity of causing the kind of movement that we need to produce the actions necessary to get the results that we want.

The conversation about leaders and leadership comes together around the question of effectiveness, and that's a major theme of this book. How do we as leaders cause the kind of movement that enables us to move beyond the increasing ineffectiveness of the industrial capitalist model that we've been living out for the last 200 years?

What does it mean to be a leader and to bring effective movement to the organization from a compassionately capitalistic point of view? As we start exploring this, the challenge is to think of these questions in the context of two roles in order to get the answers to emerge. One is the role of the formal leader. The second are the informal leaders in the system—those without title and who often hold more power than the formal leader; and that will also include the consumer. What kinds of movement are the consumers causing? They are causing and have the power to cause organizations to shift the way that they approach things.

Some recent research from the annual *Good Purpose Global Study* by Edelman in New York indicates that consumers, particularly Millennials, are causing companies to reevaluate how they conduct business through their purchasing preferences. More than 7,000 consumers, ages 18 to 64, were surveyed in 13 countries for the study. The top-line result was fascinating: 87 percent of those surveyed said that corporations should place the interests of society on at least equal footing with making a profit. Additionally, the study indicates that when quality and price are essentially perceived as being equal, social purpose becomes the deciding purchase factor.

Business vs. Society
87% globally believe business should place at least equal weight on business and society

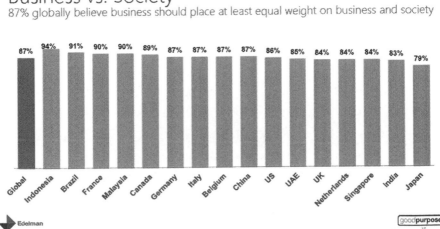

88

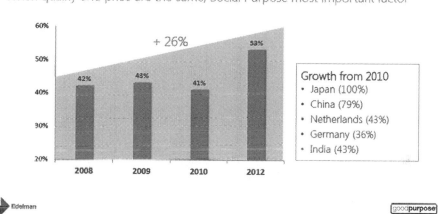

Social Purpose as Purchase Trigger
When quality and price are the same, Social Purpose most important factor

Growth from 2010
- Japan (100%)
- China (79%)
- Netherlands (43%)
- Germany (36%)
- India (43%)

Edelman · goodpurpose

With that as a backdrop, we must ask: What are some of the elements that cause coordinated movement? We think foremost among them is the notion and the nature of authenticity. This is such an important area that Blaine was asked to develop and teach a leadership program focused on authenticity for the American Association for Physician Leadership (AAPL). As a consequence of the numerous changes to the health care environment wrought by Obamacare many physicians found themselves ill-prepared to lead effectively in the new eco-sphere. The program was originally part of a larger Harvard based Meta-Leadership certification formerly offered by AAPL and is still being taught by him as part of AAPL's core leadership development offering.

David tells us a story that highlights the difference between the unconditional versus hypocritical conversation:

"Authenticity is truly directed toward value, and what happens is we have this disconnect between good intentions and actions. The larger the organization or the efforts of the movements, the more hypocritical the leader seems to be, because we can take an instance and equate it to the larger, greater purpose of what the leader intends to do. The leader in a compassionately capitalistic system has to be purely authentic and has to be evaluated for the efforts as a whole.

There is a great saying that I learned as a young leader when I was trying to please the CEO of a phone company. And I was also trying to please the Board of Directors, my executive staff, my management staff, the employees, and the consumers.

According to the old adage, "If you try to please everyone, you'll end up pleasing no one." The difficulty I encountered in trying to make everyone happy led me to realize: "I'd rather people not like me for who I am, than like me for who I'm not." My true intentions are to help others and create value, and I trust the universe will repay me accordingly. The more value I create, the more I will receive. The advantage to that, like all these other corporations that we've illustrated, is that the value will go to everyone and specifically to have a long, thriving life rather than a life of scarcity and constant struggle.

We want to learn and direct all our coordination, movement, and awareness toward creating value and being authentic to the value that we are creating — for all, not just for the board, not just for the executives, not just for the management, not just for the employees, but also for the consumer. When we create the coordination of being an authentic leader, we will automatically balance this by being true to that value.

Years ago, when people asked about my exit strategy, or my career plan, I'd say that I had two authentic values. One: I need to stay in business tomorrow; and two: I need to increase shareholder value and direct it toward the shareholders to serve a greater purpose, that is inclusive of everyone.

When I was no longer a sports agent, for example, with Warren Moon and his help, I wanted to create an authentic environment that had three purposes: To make a lot of money, to help a lot of people, and to have a lot of fun. I have yet to find anyone who as a compassionate capitalist, doesn't want those three things, those objectives, to happen. The reason is if you can make a lot of money, help a lot of people, and have a lot of fun, all at the same time, you will have an abundant backboned company and you will be an abundant leader."

We've read the encyclical letter, "*Laudato Si* of the Holy Father Francis on Care for Our Common Home" that Pope Francis issued in May 2015.[29] There is an interesting framing that he uses in the encyclical that is consistent with compassionate capitalism from the perspective that everything is interconnected. What this speaks to in terms of the traditional value set is that organizations will typically view resources as valuable within the context of how they can best be used to produce their goals and realize their objectives. That is how value is typically assigned to a resource. What that does not make room for is a fundamental truth that everything has an intrinsic value in and of itself simply as a consequence of its existence. By this we mean that everything is the expression of a consciousness giving it form – literally, every exterior has an interior. We dive much more deeply into this concept in the final chapter.

To honor the intrinsic value that something has speaks to how a compassionate leader in a compassionate capitalistic organization actually approaches the acquisition, utilization, and disposal of resources and the creation of value. It is this idea that everything has an intrinsic value imbued within it simply as a consequence of it being, which needs to be honored and attended to.

Shareholders have value no more or less than any other stakeholder. Indeed, all stakeholders intrinsically have no more or no less value than any other stakeholders in the entire organization's universe. This notion is nothing short of revolutionary. It expands the definition of stakeholder into some very interesting areas. For example, it is possible to consider the environment as a stakeholder in the business. All this comes into play within the context of compassionate capitalism, and part of this also includes just how the leaders will see themselves as leaders. This speaks directly to the notion of authenticity.

When I look in the mirror, do I like who I see? Will I follow who I see looking back at me? These are intriguing questions. Does that person know who they are? Does he or she have a well-defined core of inclusive values that informs decisions? These questions speak to the core of authenticity. We all have stories about our lives. We all have stories of who we are. We have stories of our life experiences and those of our families, friends, and cultures that have shaped us. Our stories are steeped in our history. They are steeped in our education. They are steeped in our experience.

The net of this is a realization that we manufacture these stories. We use the word "manufacture" here to drive home a point. These stories become created. Because they are created, they are never absolutely true! They are interpretations of what has occurred. But we act as if they are real and we end up behaving as if they are true. We say, "That's just the way I am." We end up leading our organizations as if the stories that we made up are carved in stone and this is the way that it is.

Being able to examine who I am becomes an important aspect of effective leadership. The Oracle of Delphi admonished seekers to "know thyself." We need to be willing to take that deep dive of exploration and discovery. Authenticity starts in the heart. Do you know yourself well enough to identify where your ground is – your ground of being? Authenticity comes from the Greek word *authentikos*, which means to be genuine. If I pay attention to being an authentic leader in a compassionately capitalistic way, my behavior will be an emotionally appropriate, significant, purposive, and responsible way of interacting with all that I'm engaging within the system. That's the difference that we as compassionate leaders can bring.

As a leader, if I look from this perspective of authenticity, I build enough trust that coordinating movement becomes less of an issue and, interestingly, because coordination is becoming more prevalent, there is less blame going on in the system about who did what or who didn't do what. The net result is that anytime blame is reduced, by definition, fear has been moved out of the system to a significant degree. And when fear is removed trust begins to build. It becomes a virtuous cycle in which things happen faster. Stephen M. R. Covey wrote a book called *The Speed of Trust: The One Thing That Changes Everything*; in it he describes an interesting tradeoff between time and money. With more trust, it takes less time for us to execute, and this actually increases the profitability of the organization. Authenticity is the key driver in this.

From a personal point of view, compassion-based authenticity also begins to build resilience. The more I know about who I am, where I am, and what I stand for, the greater is my ability to bounce back. I increasingly have the ability to hang in there a little bit longer than I typically would if the presence of trust was questionable. Resilience is built on trust as well.

Responsibility is the ability to respond. Unfortunately, for many individuals, responsibility has become confused with blame. This learning occurs early in childhood when Mom or Dad comes into the room where a lamp has been knocked off the table and asks, "Who's responsible for this?" Similar scenarios are repeated many times and we end up with an equivalency link in our minds between blame and responsibility. This sets up us and our organizations to avoid responsibility at all costs. Ask who wants to take responsibility for a project and watch people back up. The ability to compassionately and authentically respond is what breaks this link and creates efficiencies and trust. When we are authentic and accountable, we have access to the amazing leverage potential of responsibility.

Part of the ability to respond in this fashion is linked to and activates the frontal lobes of the brain in a different way. We actually make fewer errors. The practice of mindfulness leads us to a greater experience of authenticity. Research has begun to show this in an interesting way from a neurological point of view. We have access to higher cognitive faculties when we take the time to connect with what is authentic in our lives.

If I take time as a leader to pause and be somewhat introspective, I may come to a place of balance that reinforces the abstract notion that everything is connected. Just that sort of pause is something that occurs in nature. If I want to know how things work, I simply need to go take a walk in nature. There's a balance that is always in play. Nature will seek stasis. Organizations are part of a larger ecosystem, and a lack of balance is a consequence of the ways many of us run our organizations. We are out of balance.

The human environment and the natural environment will deteriorate together or they will grow together. When we consider the "human environment", there is a lot of degradation going on . . . and its consequence is evidenced in the physical environment—as it is within, so it is without. Part of this has to do with the lack of recognition from an authenticity point of view that we're all connected. When we say all connected, it's not just people who are connected. It's everything that's connected. The kind of coordinated movement that compassionate leaders engender is predicated on an increase in this awareness. And because awareness increases our choice-making capacity, we and our organizations actually become more resourceful and better positioned to thrive and not just survive when we find ways to become more aware.

How can we be effective in our roles as leaders in a compassionately capitalistic organization? As we approach compassion as an economic model, we are just beginning to think of this as a greater and more inclusive paradigm. Compassion as part of an economic model affects the choices that determine our behavior. We move away from behaviors based on a model steeped in roles of hierarchy, mindless consumerism, and exploitation toward a system evidenced by roles such as valued stakeholders, socially responsible consumers, and stewards. Organizations and individuals experience being connected and honoring the status conferred by an intimate belonging. Compassion is an economic model and it has the power to bring humans together. We think humankind, in the noblest definition of that word, is an amazing possibility. That, we think, is the challenge for the compassionate leader, to find ways to bring humans together by using their businesses as a mechanism to achieve this. You can think of the leader as the holder of this higher idealized state.

One way to visualize this is through the metaphor of a merchant as a priest. The word priest is derived from the Greek *presbýteros* which simply means elder. The meaning of priest to which we ascribe in this context has no religious connotations. It is simply that of a merchant acting in the role of an elder and who serves as a mediating agent between humans and what we are calling consciousness in order to ensure the actions taken by the business are a compassionate analog to the inspiration to act. The "merchant priests" transact their business, their spiritual business, in the field of commerce. By holding this higher state of what's possible, of interconnectedness, of honoring of intrinsic value in the way that they guide and conduct business, this compassionate merchant priest leader can have an incredible impact on the way the rest of the world actually experiences its possibility for connection and living. This goes back to our notion of value—I get to experience being fully and joyfully alive as a consequence of being in the presence of the product or service that this organization is offering. Do you as a leader engender that same experience in others when they are in your presence?

There are leaders of significant organizations today who understand this notion, both in terms of the responsibility *and* the opportunity. Their "work" begins with being able to position themselves in this context first and then their organizations follow as a consequence of this as part of a compassionate conversation. Entrepreneur Sir Richard Branson's B-team, in part, was founded as an option to jumpstart this conversation about compassionate capitalism and conscious capitalism. Branson and his team are a part of the Business Alliance for the Future that Blaine cofounded with business alliances from around the world.

These "merchant priests" are present today in businesses large and small. Paul Polman, the CEO of Unilever, approaches his position with corporate social responsibility as a key focus as evidenced by their Sustainable Living Plan. According to a Unilever spokesperson, "Unilever believes that businesses that put sustainability at the heart of their business model can grow profitably and make a positive contribution to society whilst protecting the planet for future generations."[30]

Howard Schultz, the CEO of Starbucks, is similarly oriented. He shocked the traditional business world by shutting down all 7,100 U.S. stores in 2008 to retrain their baristas and, at a cost of $30 million, brought 10,000 store managers to New Orleans to build morale. Interestingly, Wall Street wasn't impressed that Schultz refused to compromise on core Starbucks principles, including providing health insurance even for temporary employees. He consistently maintains that doing otherwise would gut what the company stands for.

Rinaldo Brutoco, founding president of the World Business Academy[31] was closely associated with Mother Teresa. The WBA is essentially a "think tank" that examines the role of business in resolving systemic problems facing society. Brutoco has consistently positioned the WBA as a champion of the notion that it's the responsibility of business to "Take Responsibility For The Whole." Almost every one of the Fellows[32] of the World Business Academy speaks in some way to this notion.

Yvon Chouinard, founder of Patagonia, built the company on his conviction that their operations and their products do no harm. In 2011 the company famously placed an ad in the *New York Times* that admonished potential customers: "Don't Buy This Jacket". The idea was that the production of the jacket had a significant environmental impact and customers buying for the sake of buying fostered unsustainable consumption. Part of the ad copy read: "There is much to be done and plenty for us all to do. Don't buy what you don't need. Think twice before you buy anything. Go to patagonia.com/commonthreads, take the Common Threads Initiative pledge and join us in the fifth R, to reimagine a world where we take only what nature can replace."[33]

Jim Sinegal, the co-founder and former CEO of Costco built the company on the philosophy that putting good treatment of employees and customers ahead of pleasing shareholders was good business. It was and is. As one of Raj Sisodia's Firms of Endearment, Costco's stock value from 1985 until Sinegal's retirement in 2012 increased by five *thousand* percent.

Kazuo Inamori, entrepreneur and Buddhist priest, has used a philosophy of focusing on happiness to establish electronics giant Kyocera Corp., create the $64 billion phone carrier now known as KDDI Corp., and rescue Japan Airlines Co. from its 2010 bankruptcy.[34]

These "merchant priests" are actually some very visible and fascinating people who recognize the power that business wields in defining and shaping how we live on and impact the planet. They are making big differences. Even the late Steve Jobs, as we'll see in the final chapter, can be considered to have been acting as a merchant priest.

The emergence of such leaders is not accidental . . . it is rooted in the conversation of authenticity. Each of these individuals (and countless others) has taken the time to look at themselves and determine what it means to be a true leader in today's world. They lead not from a command-and-control dimension, but from the point of view that we each have a responsibility (both fiscally and morally) to act as if we are all connected and that we are stewards of the resources that we're given. Everything has an intrinsic value in and of itself. Just by its existence it is valuable. We can have access to the utility surrounding it, but to unsustainably consume, despoil it and throw it away is immoral and wrong.

Which brings us to how leaders coordinate a movement. We are looking here, in part, at beginning to shift the course concerning the directive nature of industrial capitalism, which has essentially become a throw-away economic model. Consumption is such a major driver of the post-industrial and industrial capitalistic models that we have to continue to produce an ever-increasing supply just to keep the engine running.

The unintended consequence of this is disposability. When we consider disposability as a part of the cost of this economic engine, it brings into awareness the fact that we are doomed to despoil because we have to use things without appreciating the intrinsic value. As a consequence, we produce without an understanding of what it means to recycle—to reclaim a portion of that intrinsic value with which the resource is imbued. What if we began producing everything—products and services—with recycling as part of our mindset?

One of the tangible benefits of doing so is an emerging appreciation of nature, a recycling machine in itself. In nature nothing is wasted or thrown away, which is the exact opposite of our current traditional assumptions about how to run businesses. The end users, when they are done with whatever they are using, are implicitly encouraged to throw it away. There is even a business term for this: "Planned obsolescence" whereby a product with moving parts is intentionally designed to fail in a relatively short period of time so the consumer will have to dispose of it and buy a new one. Not recycle it – just throw it away.

We've always wondered, where is *away?* When we throw something away, where does it go? It doesn't have an opportunity to become recycled, because recycling is not part of the design process. A specific example of this is the use of plastics. Plastic has become one of the world's most popular materials, combining amazing functionality and low production cost. Its use has increased 20-fold in the past 50 years and is expected to double again in the next 20 years. The consequence of producing without consideration for end-use disposal is that the World Economic Forum (WEF) estimates that by the year 2050, there will be more plastic by weight in the oceans of the world than all the fish in the world's oceans combined!

As of this writing, only 14 percent of plastic packaging is collected for recycling. The reuse rate is terrible compared to other materials—58 percent of paper and up to 90 percent of iron and steel gets recycled. "After a short first-use cycle, 95% of plastic packaging material value, or $80–120 billion annually, is lost to the economy," the WEF said in a report.[35] It estimates that by 2050, the amount of plastics produced globally will increase three times to 1,124 million tons. By then, the "plastics economy" will take up 15 percent of the world's global carbon budget, compared to just 1 percent in 2014. The so-called carbon budget is the total amount of carbon dioxide the world can pump into the atmosphere while still having a chance of stopping short of 2 degrees Celsius of global warming.

The WEF reported that the only way to avoid a disaster is to massively improve the economics and uptake of recycling. That means giving people incentives to collect plastic garbage and recycle, use reusable packaging, and encourage countries to drastically improve their waste collection infrastructure, to avoid plastic garbage leaking into nature. How do we coordinate the movement to do this?

Compassionate leaders take into account these questions with the end point of usability in mind when considering how their products and services are designed. The end point is where the consumer is finished with the product. How does business design, and build into pricing, ways that the consumer can naturally take the disposed materials back to the ecosystem in a generative fashion—in a way that reclaims the intrinsic value that was there to begin with?

That's a process that honors intrinsic values or the components that went into the creation of that resource or service to begin with. These generate different questions that leaders offer their organizations as focal points for coordination. How do we coordinate around these new sets of questions? How do we coordinate around these "new sensibilities"? Awareness begins to precede the creation of different choices. When we do this as leaders, we become responsible for creating cultures that will allow for these seeds to germinate and take hold.

Cultures are seedbeds. Years ago, Ford president Mark Fields, based on work by management consultant Peter Drucker, said, "Culture will eat strategy for breakfast." I don't care how extraordinary your idea is, if the culture in your organization doesn't support its growth, the best idea in the world will die. It's like throwing seeds onto a desert gravel bed.

We look to reinforce the ideals of compassionately capitalistic leaders who have the idea of experiencing and providing value without there being waste. If you shift the paradigm to one of providing value (instead of getting for something it), the universe, the system, and the culture itself fills that value. If I create something of value, I'm utilizing every aspect of each component with consideration to its full lifetime. I'm not just thinking of a product that I can get more value for than it cost me to produce. This is where these great leaders see beyond the scope and scale of what most people can create.

We'll give a brief example. Absorbent Designs LLC came up with a U-shaped towel design (the iTowel) that fits better over the shoulder for certain sports. It's a terrific design. Because the CEO is a compassionate leader, the company utilizes all the resources it has to create value. In the end, everything is completely recycled, whether it is metal, plastic, or paper. The company is a valuable organization led by an authentic leader who looked at the product as being part of a whole value chain that included customer experience *and* product disposal/recycling, trusting that everything would be utilized to create that value. In this culture, people who produce the product have taken recycling into consideration when they start, sustain, and grow the business.

That's a perfect example of what it means to create coherence out of complexity. There is so much noise from media and from the ubiquitous access to information and so much need for speed that the complexities, at times, seem completely overwhelming. Sometimes, shortcuts are taken with the aim to get this product out quickly without a consideration for the long-term impact it creates.

The alternative is a kind of mindfulness, authenticity, and clarity about who we are as interconnected elements within a larger ecosystem. That allows us to design in a manner that doesn't become onerous— something that makes us feel we're slowing ourselves down to do it. Paradoxically, it actually speeds us up over the long term because we don't have to worry about, "Did we do this well?" We don't have to go back and reiterate it.

Recyclability is not an issue at that point in time. It is already built into the design or the process or the product. That is an important piece of authenticity. It allows us to enter and create the experience of flow. Authenticity is a flow-inducing state, both for the organization and for the individual.

This flow state arises from the contextual distinction between abundance versus scarcity. As we've described, a company that is afraid of not going to market fast enough is actually in the grip of a scarcity consciousness that is contraction inducing and the "speed" of movement is experienced as frenetic rather than flowing. Instead, when a company shifts its paradigm toward abundance, speed is an asset that is viewed (and experienced) as being abundantly available and in which it can further create more value and abundance. Movement is not driven by a threat or fear or a scarce energy. When threat, fear, and scarcity are present, it is inevitable that people will tend to create more waste and less sustainability.

There is a famous "sleight of tongue" statement that renowned psychiatrist Milton Erickson used to employ. He'd invite his clients to "Take as much time as you need within the next ten minutes to answer my question." Exploring how we can "take as much time as we need within the next three-month design cycle to innovate" is an interesting way to approach the process!

When organizations and individuals and teams are in a flow state, the experience of time stops. You look up and ask, "Where did the time go?" We have the experience of being out of time in the truest and most generative sense of the phrase. It's not "out of time" in the sense of a scarce commodity or resource that we don't have enough of. We move our organizations and ourselves from an awareness that time is an infinite resource when we are in that authentic state.

Have you ever heard the saying, "Deadlines create voids?" If we impose a deadline, we are actually putting an artificial and limiting context onto time because meeting the deadline requires that everything happens in the right way, in the correct sequence, and at the perfect time. Perfection becomes the default orientation, which invites the dominance of a command-and-control mentality. If we are focused instead on doing the job in the most efficient, effective, and ultimately successful way, then we actually don't need deadlines, because the process is going to happen in the most abundant way. All we are focusing on is doing the job. The minute we put a deadline on something, we create a sense of panic, a feeling of pressure, and a fear of failure.

It's like trying to win the lottery. Everything has to fall into place perfectly in order to do so. It's almost impossible to just come up with all six winning numbers at the exact right time and space that are coming up on the machine. When we create/impose a deadline, we create the same obstacles of void and shortage by saying, "This needs to be done by Friday". We automatically create scarcity and waste because it will almost never be done "right". If we focus on what needs to be accomplished, it might be done on Wednesday and Thursday or it might be finished on Saturday or Sunday. Regardless, we want that value. We don't want an artificial placement of a deadline to be the norm in organizations—far from being a positive motivator, deadlines actually produce fear and contraction in systems.

This speaks directly to the great destructive nature of quarterly results. Those sorts of metrics are counter to what is true in nature. Nature is an exemplar of what connection produces. Nature can't and won't be managed. Management is the hubris of a consciousness of separation. Nature doesn't work from quarterly results. Yes, we have a calendar cycle that allows us to appreciate when summer and fall are likely to make their appearances, but ecosystems don't pay attention to the calendar, they just move gradually through these natural cycles. We'd be hard-pressed to make a declaration that summer has just turned the corner and it is now fall, if we didn't have a calendar to pay attention to. We know it intuitively because we live in it at that point in time. That is part of the nature of flow.

When we look at this, authenticity makes it possible for us to connect our businesses to a life force that allows for what has already been created to manifest itself in an appropriate time, space, and way. These dynamics are a fascinating approach to orient the organization, and it begins, if it's practiced well, to drive stress out of the system. When we say drive stress out of the system, we're not talking about necessary stimulus. We're talking about the unnecessary chronic stress that has been introduced by artificial stimulus into just about every system that has been artificially created. It is an artificial, continuous, chronic stress that reduces our ability to live fully, that reduces our ability to be creative, and that has the presence of fear running through it all the time. Fear is a function of separation. Authenticity is the antithesis of separation. Authenticity is a hallmark of compassion.

Authentic leaders are those who are continually finding ways to "wake up". They are looking for possibility and probability. They are paying attention to *sensation,* which is the litmus test for connection. How does it feel? Contrary to what many people think, feelings have an integral place in business. Feelings have a box seat, if you will. Feelings need to have a position of prime importance in business. We need to learn to appreciate and develop feelings in business, and we mean feelings not from the point of view of emotions that are based on assessing something as right/wrong or good/bad. Rather feelings based on sensing "Is this working or not working"?

Sensational assessments (for example, hot/cold, tight/loose, smooth/rough, pleasing/noxious) occur before feelings arise; chronic feeling states produce emotions. The distinctions between working/not working and good/bad or right/wrong are important to appreciate. Good/bad or right/wrong have no sensational analog—they are emotional assessments that are rooted in beliefs of what "should/shouldn't be". Working/not working have specific sensational analogs that have not been hijacked by beliefs and transformed into emotions. We can attribute working/not working to certain feelings in our business in relation to the quality of our products and services; certain feelings in our body about how we are being successful. You might call this paying attention to your intuition or gut rather than the dictates of an economic or business model.

A good example of this are the disastrous consequences of the structural adjustment programs (SAPs) imposed on emerging economies by the World Bank and the International Monetary Fund (IMF). In his book *Race Against Time: Searching for Hope in AIDS-Ravaged Africa,* Stephen Lewis (United Nations special envoy for HIV/AIDS in Africa) details how in the face of obvious failures, the IMF and the World Bank continued to insist on imposing draconian and ideologically "correct" terms on emerging economies (specifically in Africa) that decimated the affected countries' abilities to deliver healthcare and education to some of the most vulnerable people on the planet.

In order to secure loans, the borrowing countries were forced to accept conditions, such as the sale of public sector corporations, macroeconomic limits on the number of people (for example, teachers and nurses) who could be hired, limits on the amount of money that could be spent on social sector needs as a percentage of the countries' GNP, and user fees for medical care and education. These were dictated in large part by blind devotion to the entrenched capitalistic model. According to Lewis, "At the heart of structural adjustment policies there lay two absolutes: Curtail and decimate the public sector; enhance, at any cost, the private sector."[36] The unwillingness or inability of the bureaucrats in charge to feel what was not working versus to assess what was going on within the context of right/wrong policy decisions was hugely contributory to the HIV/AIDS pandemic on the African continent and resulted in an infrastructure collapse from which large parts of Africa have yet to recover. In his insightful book, *The End of Poverty: Economic Possibilities for Our Time*, Professor of Economics Jeffrey D. Sachs goes into great detail about the significance of not feeling the consequences of economic policies.

All this begins to move us into the notion of being awake, being mindful, being intentional, and paying attention to what's working and not working. Paying attention to connection. Paying attention to how things are being produced from ideation, through production and delivery and into the disposal phase. This is a part of what it means to be compassionate—which is a consequence of being awake—and is instrumental to causing coordinated movements through the system. It is not just knee-jerk action.

It is coordinated movement throughout the lifecycle of the service or process or product and is a function of intention. It is coordinated movement through the way the teams interact, and through the aggregation and utilization of resources. All of this is coordination moving in relationships. Everything is about relationships. Relationships speak to connections, and that's what compassion is about. We are compassionately connected to everything in the ecosphere in which we do business.

We think that connection is also defined by relativity—specifically our *relative* relationships with time and all people and all things in space. It enables authenticity and increases accountability when we realize and act as if we are, ourselves, part of an indivisible whole. And as we seek to create value for ourselves, we thereby create value for the whole. It is a shift in the pervading model of capitalism that is much more holistic and compassionate than, "I must take from the whole in order to survive."

Essentially what compassion and authenticity are enabled by is a consequence of this indivisible sense of "we" as the nature of love or truth. Like feelings, love belongs in business. Love or truth is a prerequisite to passion and to its counterpart, compassion. I love what I do. I love what I'm doing to and with the market. I love the way that people feel—specifically, how they feel when they are in the presence of our services or products. Money can buy a dog, but only love can make it wag its tail!

Love or truth is an integral part of both compassionate capitalism and compassionate leadership. How we define love in the context of compassionate capitalism is important. We don't refer here to romantic love or to the emotion typically associated with love. Rather, love as we are defining it has to do with intrinsic value. When I love in the manner we reference, I grant you the right to grow and develop to your fullest potential. My services and/or products are offered in support of this growth. This is the root of value in the compassionate capitalism model. You have, our products/services have, the resources used in their production all have, intrinsic value that we honor and nurture.

All business on this planet occurs within a closed ecosphere. We can think of Earth in the context of Gaia (the ancient Greek name for Earth) which suggests that this ecosystem we inhabit is a living, sentient system. The *Gaia hypothesis* proposes that organisms interact with their inorganic surroundings on Earth to form a synergistic self-regulating, complex system that helps to maintain and perpetuate the conditions for life on the planet.[37] The hypothesis was first formulated in the 1970s by chemist James Lovelock and co-developed by microbiologist Lynn Margulis. In 2006, the Geological Society of London awarded Margulis the Wollaston Medal, its highest award, in part for his work on the Gaia hypothesis. The earth literally breathes and has its own electromagnetic field (the Schumann resonances[38]) that is not unlike the electromagnetic field that surrounds all matter on the planet.

We can view the human being as part of the microbiome of a larger Gaia organism. Your body is made up of around ten trillion cells, but you harbor a hundred trillion bacteria in your gut—your microbiome. Essentially, for every gene in your genome, there are 100 bacterial ones and these comprise your microbiome. According to Wikipedia, "the microbiome of the gut has been characterized as a 'forgotten organ,' and the possibility has been raised that "the mammalian immune system, which seems to be designed to control microorganisms, is in fact controlled by microorganisms."[39] Just the same as with the microbiome in our guts, if we are not attending to the overall health of Gaia's microbiome, it begins to affect the entire rest of the body.

An ecosystem, in the way we reference it here, speaks to the immediate system of interrelated and interdependent components that comprise our organization and ourselves as a part. This is the tangible piece of time and space that we can see and feel around us, containing all that we think we have the most immediate impact on. The system exists within a larger system, and that system exists within an even larger system, and every part of the macro system is interconnected, and all encompassed by the ecosphere.

The compassionate capitalist is an authentic leader, and authenticity in part speaks the truth, and that opens a whole conversation about what truth is. The notion of "truth" is not absolute. Rather it is rooted in the experience of authenticity, and authenticity in the way that we are defining it has to be interconnected. A possible truth that we are going to build a compassionate business as part of an economic model lives within a truth that we are all connected. What is happening out there is happening in here, and vice versa. We live in an interconnected, relationship-defined ecosphere.

If I throw something away, there is a part of me that I'm throwing away. There is a part of my business that I'm throwing away. If I'm accounting for it in the context of "This thing has intrinsic value in and of itself and it is connected to me," I am going to care for it; I am going to honor it. By definition it infers that I am also going to care for and honor every part of who we are as a business.

That honoring and caring for then translates into how the people in the organization feel. It informs the way that the culture of the organization actually forms itself. This isn't about singing *Kumbaya*. It's not about sitting around the campfire and everybody is in agreement and eating s'mores. It's about making hard choices. It's about minimizing or even eliminating "tradeoffs" as a viable option.

There is obviously much room for conflict here. How that conflict is actually addressed is key. Metaphors that are useful when welcoming conflict are to think about it is as carbon under pressure producing a diamond. Or steel rubbing against steel that makes sparks but it sharpens the blade. Conflict is not excluded from compassionate capitalism. We believe it to be actually a core requirement.

Leaders bring conflict to the surface. They don't avoid it. They might actually make space in the culture for conflict to surface so that assumptions can be ironed out. Your assumption and my assumption about what is real today and what is necessary today are both valid. They need to be vetted in the light of day so we can find a collaborative and coordinated way to move ourselves forward. If my primary focus is that my point of view is more right than yours, that causes each of us to defend our respective opinions and the net result is less opportunity for coordinated movement.

This coordinated movement does not mean that conflict has been eradicated. Coordinated movement needs conflict as a healthy component of every systemic dynamic. In order for the system to run well, that conflict needs to be surfaced so that the machine that we are as an organization functions well. We say "machine" not to de-humanize, but because our organizations have integrated parts that work together. They have to know and be aware of where the rub points are (thus the importance of sensation-based feelings) so they can be "lubricated" by intentional conversations to actually work more cohesively and more harmoniously together. Each unique element of the organization is going to have its own role, its own responsibility, and its own orientation and focus.

If coordination is occurring well, room has been made for honoring and realizing that your point of view is an aspect of my point of view that I just haven't recognized yet. I might not want to validate it. I might not want to hold it as being true today, but it is still a valid point. If we can see that your point of view is as valid to you as mine is to me, then we can move forward. It lends itself to more harmony and political discourse. It ultimately lends itself to more compassion and harmony in doing commerce.

All these things come into play when we approach leadership from this orientation. Our role as leaders is to create the conditions for coordinated movement by increasing awareness, by acting as if, from a merchant-priest orientation, we are the caretaker of the higher spiritual existence that all can aspire to live into. Business becomes a spiritual process involving continual awakening, and the running of business then becomes a spiritual discipline.

This positioning takes us full circle back to authenticity, where moving and living and acting and leading from a position of authenticity requires a spiritual orientation. It requires a realization that everything is connected. We continually keep finding ways to honor those connections and strive to find ways to bring them into conversations, either objectively or subjectively, in the ways that we work together and run our businesses.

Leaders must come to the table ready to practice these ideas. This is one of those things that business leaders such as Sir Richard Branson and Paul Polman do so well. We continually look for ways that we can practice, and, in the practicing, we more acutely notice. And in the noticing, we pay attention to the sensations of what works and what doesn't work and we make adjustments. A simple truism is that "We don't rise to the level of our expectations; we fall to the level of our practices." We want to be in a position as leaders to continually elevate the practices we and our organizations are engaged in. That is an essential function of consciousness and of mindfulness.

CHAPTER 6

The Compassionate Capitalist as A Leader

"You never change things by fighting the existing reality.
To change things build a new model that makes
the existing model obsolete."
-- Buckminster Fuller

We believe that all effective leaders have and exhibit compassion. This doesn't mean that they are soft. In fact, they are often very steely and pragmatic. For many leaders aspiring to become more effective, the challenge is in knowing how to shift the paradigm or the perspective in order to create value in a way that transcends both ourselves and a sole focus on material gain.

David came out of law school and business school and quickly become what many would call a successful businessman, a successful capitalist, but not an effective leader. As the vice president of sales in one of his first businesses, his goal was to get as much value as he could from those he worked with and for. His primary focus was not dissimilar to that of many of his peers. It revolved around how he could get paid as much as possible from his employer and/or how he could get as much as he could from his prospects, associates, and the consumers.

The old capitalistic system is based on that scarce mental attitude that there isn't enough and that you need to get as much as possible while giving up as little as possible. That included techniques like overselling, back-end selling, being duplicitous when necessary to close a deal, revealing shades of the truth, all the methodologies that we think are iconic within who we perceive to be leaders. Living in this context creates scarcity, cynical thinking, even hatred and jealousy. This type of leader believes you must be a shrewd business person lest you not get your due.

David had financial success in his 20s, retired in his 30s, having used these "normal" values that typify the old paradigm and the attitudes of a traditional captain of industry leader to achieve his financial goals. Through his emerging understanding of the idea of value in the way we describe it, and after learning to be a compassionate capitalist, he transformed himself. In doing so, he had to purge himself of all his financial wealth and recreate himself in an authentic way. Here's how:

> "The way I did that was by utilizing four pillars of truth that allowed me to have a sound perspective of true value. Instead of focusing on how much value I can *get*, I started over with this authentic being who believes that I am here to *create* as much value as I can. I trust that everything else will come to meet me at this level of true value. That everything else will end up at a value of what I provide and I don't have to go out and take value from people. I discovered that if I consistently provide value, and the more value I provide, this vessel that is my being will be filled with authentic value. The only way to do that is to consistently be your authentic self. You can't hide from the truth and it won't hide from you!

> Several revelations come to mind that I've been told throughout this transformation. One, I was a pleaser. I wanted everyone to love me. I wanted to be diplomatic in every sense. I felt that was the key to being a leader, a capitalist. In a capitalistic society, everyone has to be happy. I'd say or do whatever it took to try and make everyone happy.

> A wise man once said, "I'd rather people hate me for who I am than love me for who I'm not, as long as I'm authentic." I agree. I've found that as long as I strive for the truth, I have nothing

to worry about. I utilize the word *strive* because I know that I am imperfect and that I still make mistakes. I just need to catch those mistakes and quickly rectify them so they don't become a consistent behavioral pattern.

A compassionate leader needs to be authentic and true. He or she has one simple rule—to provide value. If your focus is to provide value in a capitalistic society, this is the key to being a compassionate leader: to teach people that they need only be concerned with providing value, and trust the universe. Trust that everything else will come to others to fill the value that you're providing.

The Four Pillars

Pillar #1 is *gratitude*. Life is meant to instruct, not obstruct. The way we perceive ourselves and others is a matter of gratitude. This pillar is essential to empowering others. If we are gracious, our past is viewed as positive, which makes our present positive and that increases the likelihood that our future will be bright! This, in essence, allows us to be authentic and happy!

Pillar #2 is *empathy*, which is also forgiveness. As leaders, we must forgive ourselves before we can forgive others. Forgiveness gives us peace; and peace provides us with awareness. Then we can be more aware and more efficient, because we're not wasting energy with criticism, insecurities, and fear.

Pillar #3 is *accountability*. Ultimately accountability is so liberating. When we are accountable, we know we are in control of everything. Once we become accountable, we live above the line formed by blame, shame, and justification. We have the power to provide value for anything that we're doing. We create our own value absent of obstacles, voids, and shortages.

Pillar #4 is *effective communication*. Today we have numerous modes of communication. We are still in the infancy stage of utilizing these different ways to communicate because they change so quickly. In the distant past, the only modes of communication were speaking, writing, and reading. We progressed to the telephone and answering machines, then computers and smartphones. We moved forward to the Web with Instagram, Snapchat, Twitter, and ever evolving modes and media of information to enhance our ways of sharing a vision.

It's not just what we say, or how we say it; it's what platform we are saying it on. The energy and context can be changed completely with the way the message is portrayed or delivered. If we're not familiar with all the modes and media of communication, and we don't know the independent and dependent variables to effectively communicate, we put ourselves at a huge detriment to being a compassionate capitalistic leader.

If we don't know how to communicate effectively to the Millennials via TV, print, radio, text, Instagram, Snapchat, Facebook, and LinkedIn, our authentic intention might be misconstrued. Therefore, we must make a commitment to utilize the four pillars as often as possible."

As compassionate leaders, we keep coming back to a foundation of authenticity, which is a quality we think of as people living into, not living up to. With this notion, there is no success or failure. It is truly an aspirational and ultimately spiritual process. We're speaking in this regard to the notion of self-mastery.

Ideally, we're always in the process of discovering more about ourselves, but this will only happen if we're willing to position ourselves to continually examine what we're doing and how we're being. The distinction that enables this is that of moving away from processes of comparison and of judgment toward a process of questioning simply whether this is working or not working. Comparison is a great place to start, but a horrible place to take up residence. As we discussed earlier, focusing on questions of working/not working takes the value-based judgment out of the equation so that we can legitimately evaluate the impact of what we're doing from the orientation of that word: impact. A legitimate, well-formed question focusing on impact is one that is free from judgment about whether this is the right way to do it or the wrong way to do it. It is also a way in which we keep ourselves present, which is a key element of self-mastery.

The process of self-mastery begins to employ those distinctions. Take for example communication. I can communicate in a lot of ways. Most leaders rely solely on the spoken word, but that's such a minimal part of the communication process. Without going into the famous studies conducted by Professor Albert Mehrabian that resulted in the often misapplied 7%-38%-55% Rule[40], suffice it to say that communication is a particularly complex undertaking and is a skill that many leaders have little mastery over. We love psychologist Virginia Satir's definition of communication: "It's the ways that we work out common meaning with one another." If we don't have common meaning, we don't have a platform from which to effect coordinated movement.

This brings us full circle back to the question of what leadership is. As stated before, it's the process of creating coordinated movement in the system that produces the actions necessary to get the results that we want. When we're looking at compassion as a platform, when we're looking at communication as a tool, then we've got something that we can behaviorally organize ourselves and our business around. The more compassion we bring to the conversation, the more we encourage the same with others, and the more authentic the entire process becomes.

This returns to the notion of how they feel, "they" meaning my followers. How do they feel about themselves when they're in my presence? There's a connective component to that question. If they feel free to explore themselves, if they feel free to voice concerns that are authentically arising in them, then we're going to have the basis for greater coordinated movement.

We want to communicate with compassionate intention. How can we engage the process with this kind of intention? It's focused on what the outcome is qualitatively. What is the value that we will create at the feeling level? That's an enormous concept, because it ultimately informs and develops the culture in which we're originating our work process. It's the culture that germinates and leads to the production of our services or our products. This is called ontological design. It's the intentional process of developing an environment that works to create the designer as an iterative mechanism.

A highly effective leader pays attention to the quality of the culture. Again, we're struck with the notion that, to paraphrase Peter Drucker in a comment attributed to Ford President and CEO Mark Fields, culture will eat the strategy, not for lunch, but for breakfast. It would eat it for lunch, but things are moving so fast that breakfast is probably more appropriate here.

A compassionate leader asks: "Am I creating a culture of awareness that causes us to become more aware? Am I creating a culture of compassion and authenticity that fosters compassion and authenticity? Am I creating a culture where coordinated movement is the litmus test for our effectiveness? Are we getting coordinated movement?

In Pope Francis' encyclical, cited previously in this book, he referenced that not only are we impacting the world as businesses, but that as a consequence of this we have a moral opportunity for impact as businesses on the quality of life on the planet. There can be no renewal of our relationship with nature without a renewal of humanity itself. We love that phrase, *a renewal of humanity itself*, and all that it entails.

That's how we end up impacting in a positive way the world in which we live. That's the opportunity for compassionate capitalism—to positively impact all life on this planet and to renew humanity itself.

Compassion and authenticity are how we accomplish that. This means recognizing that I am connected, that we are all connected, with all life on this planet, and that our movements have consequences. That the way we source and use resources makes a difference. How we aggregate resources to produce a product with the intention of having it be disposable on the backside in order to make it renewable makes it possible to create a virtuous cycle.

These are some of the things that we pay attention to. It leads us toward a focus on sustainability not only as a way to mitigate climate impact, but also as a way to lead social transformation, to connect us to the notion of making a difference, to renew our relationship with nature, which is ultimately a conversation of sustainability.

In the way that we define it here, sustainability is about developing the capacity to continually start over. It's not an evergreen sort of a thing. It is, in fact, an iterative process. "Dean of Personal Development" Earl Nightingale defined success as "the progressive realization of a worthy goal or ideal." Success isn't a linear model. There's a cyclical end to something that causes the renewal of something else. That focus on sustainable success – developing the capacity to continually start over – provides the antidote to the fear of loss.

The notion of a consciousness of abundance is offered in a context that recognizes we live in a world of finite resources and appreciating that it's an infinitely abundant energetic universe. We actually live on a planet that's in a universe of such abundant energy that if we're using our resources well—with compassion—life will be well. Energy can never be destroyed. It's always transmuted. It's always transformed through utilization. We're looking at how we continue to do that, and the answer is with compassionate intention.

We can evaluate the effectiveness of compassionate leaders according to how they communicate with resources. And how they communicate with individuals, or with their market, from an orientation of sustainability. How well do they lead the process of social transformation with their business?

A great example of this is illustrated by Daily Table. The company is a not-for-profit retail grocery that, according to their website, offers their customers a variety of tasty, convenient, and affordable foods that will help them "...feel and be your best; food that will keep you moving forward, not hold you back. We provide both 'grab-n-go' ready to eat meals, and a selection of produce, bread, dairy and grocery items all at prices that will put a smile on your face, and designed to fit within every budget. Many of our items are prepared fresh daily in our own kitchen onsite."[41] While at first glance this may not sound revolutionary it truly is.

Doug Rauch founded the organization in 2015. Doug worked at specialty foods retailer Trader Joe's for 35 years – 14 of them as President. In addition to his role as Founder and President at Daily Table he's also on the Board of Directors and serves as CEO of Conscious Capitalism. According to Doug, Daily Table was founded to address the fact that there are over 49 million Americans who are food insecure or go hungry. That statistic represents one for every six Americans. From Doug's perspective it is "...morally wrong that one in six Americans can't afford to eat well in the richest nation in the history of the world." Essentially, what the statistics point to is that this population represents mostly the working poor who are forced to buy food that is basically unhealthy. Food that is calorically dense but nutritionally stunted. The result is skyrocketing diabetes, obesity, and heart disease amongst a population that cannot afford to become ill. In Doug's words this is "a healthcare cost tsunami" that will, and is, inhibiting us as a society.

In researching the problem, Doug discovered that 30-40 percent of everything that is grown in America is never consumed...rather it's wasted. His great insight was to link these two facts. Literally, he wanted to "use one problem—all this wasted food—to solve another problem, which is the unaffordability of nutrients. That's the fruits, the vegetables, the dairy, the protein that people "should be eating and can't afford" to replace the "high fructose corn syrup and heavily processed foods that they can afford." He founded Daily Table to face the problem of wasted food by providing low-priced, affordable nutrition within a business model that is uniquely structured to address a major hurdle with charitable giving.

Although it is legally a non-profit organization, Daily Table compassionately and consciously moved away from being run as a charity. Their goal is to effectively raise "funds" BY the delivery of their mission (via sales) instead of the traditional model of raising funds FOR the delivery of their mission. This is a focus that makes a substantial difference.

One of Doug's realizations early on was that charitable giving has a built-in problem. It is the power differential between the donor and the recipient. There is a giver and a "needer". The saintliest of intentions doesn't mitigate this. It's never a relationship of equals. However, in the marketplace the customer is the one with the power. Doug says, "In a system with voluntary exchange, the customer is free to shop wherever they want to shop and to buy whatever they want to buy. Because they hold the power of the purse they have an inherent sense of power which then also gives a sense of dignity. Many people who are in tremendous need won't use the services of a soup kitchen or a food bank because of the loss of dignity. They are too proud. They are ashamed."

Daily Table has been designed around using a capitalistic model to deliver this basic human need for dignity. According to Doug, "One of my big learnings was that people are even hungrier to keep their dignity than their health. And hence, they will go without if they feel they had to give up their dignity or do something demeaning to get their needs met. So, Daily Table had to ask, 'How do we hit on all fronts?'"

For Daily Table, the value proposition became how to ensure that the customer felt delighted to be alive while in the presence of their product! The question Doug and his team wrestled with was how do we get food that would otherwise be wasted delivered in a manner that provides a dignified solution so that people feel better? And, how do they do so in a manner that is economically sustainable?

Part of the answer came when they took time to explore the nature of poverty. Rather than simply assuming it was solely a function of income, further research suggested that those lower down on the economic ladder also faced what could be termed a poverty of time. These are typically people working more than one job while juggling the considerable demands of just living life. This realization led Doug and his team to conclude that their primary competition would not be other grocery outlets. Rather, their primary competition was fast food outlets. They quickly concluded that Daily Table was going to have to provide ready-made, grab-and-go meals so their customers could come in, shop and take home in two to three minutes a nutritious meal for their family. This is now over fifty percent of their sales.

Moving from "managing the probable" to "leading into the possible" requires us to address challenges in a fundamentally different way. For Doug and his team at Daily Table this looks like, in his words, "A good life starts with good health. If you don't have good health, it's really tough to go out and have a great life. Health starts with a good diet. You can't eat decade after decade of junk and expect it not to affect your body or your mind. So, we owe it to the kids, to our citizens, the world to try to provide healthy meals, to provide a healthy outcome, so they can go off and have a great life and all of us get to do and be our best and not be held back by limitations because simply by diet it could've been avoided."

We find these two things – managing the probable and leading into the possible – tied together when we approach leading our businesses with compassion. As we go through our own personal transformation as business leaders, we note that when we approach the process from an orientation of compassion it has a profound impact on what we view as potential. In a spiritual sense, as a compassionate leader, we teach about the field of intention and the field of potentiality. These two things are closely related. Not only do we have to focus our intent, but we must look at the potential and the realistic, pragmatic execution of its manifestation.

That's why compassionate capitalists, in our opinion, are best suited for this authentic type of leadership. They can draw from the field of intention, the field of potentiality, and bring it back to a pragmatic business application that is filtered through 250 years of involvement with capitalism. To make it pragmatic to others is to make it valuable.

That field of potentiality is about consciousness. A compassionate leader is a conscious leader, and a leader of emerging consciousness. Leadership is the art of making the possible visible to the point that it becomes probable. In one sense, everything that ever existed or ever will exist has already been "created" as a possibility in consciousness. It is simply awaiting the right time and circumstances to manifest as a probability. It's about manifesting what already exists as unrealized potential.

Anything that has ever been invented that we can touch, feel, sense, or taste was essentially invented twice. First as an idea, then in material form. It's the manifestation of that ideation that we bring to play here, the ability to conceptualize in a holistic way that allows us to move to a place of manifestation. It's already created – it exists – as a possibility. Now we look toward manifesting it in a way that allows us to impact this material world in which we live in a different, more altruistic way.

Intellectual artist Leonardo da Vinci is generally credited with "inventing" the helicopter. The design for his helicopter was drawn in 1493, 450 years before an actual helicopter would take to the air. Of course, what was missing at the time was the means that would allow his idea to take form. Today's helicopter had to wait for material science to produce metal (aluminum) that is both strong and lightweight. It also waited for the development of engines that would have a high power-to-weight ratio. The engines also had to be efficient enough to allow for a manageable amount of fuel to be carried, while yielding enough energy out of the fuel to power it. From idea (possibility) to form (probability)—450 years!

This is where intention, consciousness, and compassion become inextricably linked. These three concepts allow us to create in a holistic way that honors life, that brings life to what we do, and that brings life to what we offer.

Consider how we define value—creating the possibility to feel more joyfully alive as a consequence of being in the presence of your service or product. We get to experience feeling delightfully alive as a consequence of touching and being touched by your product or service. We can bring this possibility to business and, by extension, to all life forms as a probability. We're being compassionate organizations that produce compassionate services and products. That's a big deal.

How does this relate to the creation of collective consciousness that organizes around compassionate capitalism? Obviously, it starts with the leader's individual consciousness. How is being a compassionate, capitalistic leader related to creating this collective consciousness? That's the ultimate intention because it moves us into the conversation—how do we create coordinated movement?

What are the elements of coordinated movement? Blaine has spent over four decades researching and developing ways to teach this to clients all over the world. One of his leadership programs that he conducts in Japan has earned an ISO certification; he developed and taught a leadership program that was a major part of Nokia's global leadership development initiative in the mid and late '90s and, as was previously mentioned, he teaches an Authentic Leadership program for the American Association for Physician Leadership. He has defined five basic competencies (Awareness, Communication, Trust, Ownership, and Context) that are typically involved in creating coordinated movement. In the Authentic Leadership model he designed and uses in work with his clients, these five competencies are developed and expressed within the larger domains of Spirit, Mind, Time/Space, and Personal Mastery.

Trust is a key part of the process that we particularly want to consider at this point. Because organizations are, as we have earlier said, essentially groups of people that are in relationship, it's important to realize that trust is the lubricant that keeps relationships functioning. Certainly, the culture in which the various pieces in the organization are moving influences it. So too are the values that we espouse. But, more importantly, the values that we practice are a huge piece of the process. Every organization has a set of either implicit or altruistic espoused values that provide the basis for an organizing principle, but it's the values in *practice* that make a difference.

Authentic, compassionate leaders are making sure (to the degree that it's consciously possible) that we exhibit values behaviorally that are consistent with what we're espousing—that our value's core is aligned with our actions and, as a consequence, is authentic. That alignment and coherence builds the trust that is vitally important.

We don't necessarily rise to the level of our expectations. As mentioned previously, we fall to the level of our practices. Every value has a behavioral analogue. What does trust look like behaviorally? Let's practice that behavior. What does love in a business look like? Let's practice that behavior. Let's identify what that behavior is and then personally practice it and insist that others in the organization practice it as well.

Are we going to get it right all the time? No, but if we're authentic, we'll recognize when we're living it and when we're missing it. We won't fall into the trap of trying to live up to an impossibly high standard that allows zero mistakes. That is a trap, because living up to something is oriented around perfection. Leading an organization from an aspiration for excellence, not perfection, allows us to aspire to excellence and encourages continual iterations based on integrating learning.

This is the distinction between something working or not working, as opposed to something being right or wrong. Right or wrong is a perfection-based notion. It will always trap us. It's a contractive conversation. Nobody likes the experience of being wrong. I understand I get to grow and develop if I can say, "Well, that was wrong. Let's see what we can do to improve." But that tends to be a short-cycled way of thinking. If I'm looking at our progress from the standpoint of working or not working, it takes me out of the value judgment that is based on a belief that there is a "right" way to do something. "This didn't work. Okay. What do I need to improve here?" That's something that I can live into.

This approach is rooted in vulnerability, which is the foundation of authenticity, and which is the path to compassion. It is what truth is. Truth is rooted in the authentically honest assessment of what is working or not working. It requires vulnerability to ask the question and to transparently examine the answer that comes back. Is this working or not working? Unfortunately, the vast majority of people on this planet would prefer being right over getting what they say they want. The need to be right is a slippery slope on which to build coordinated movement. The need to be right is avoided or at least acknowledged by a compassionate capitalist. But it's a driving factor for an industrial capitalist.

The process of inquiry doesn't necessarily look for any "right" answer. It is an exploration. What answers are possible? That's part of the process of self-mastery. How do I lead myself? I'm always growing. I'm always expanding. I'm always shifting and changing. The need to be right is often rooted in the need for predictability and stability.

When we consider the distinction between management and leadership, *management* is fundamentally preoccupied with predictability and stability. The metrics, structures, and processes of organizations are then designed around stability and predictability. *Leadership* causes movement. By definition, leadership is not stable. It is often chaotic. It causes things to shift. It causes us to move into territories we've never explored or traversed.

To do that authentically, with passion, with compassion, we need to let go of being right, and be willing to just explore and delight in what appears. This is where the question of working/not working becomes relevant. That's what we use to keep ourselves on track, to keep our organization on track.

In today's postindustrial capitalist world, it's irrefutably obvious that how we conduct business is not working. We need to do things differently. That something different speaks directly to renewing our relationship with nature by renewing humanity itself, renewing how we, as individuals, hold ourselves. We are evolving and we need to have compassion as we engage in that evolutionary process.

Sustainable success, as we've said, is about developing the capacity to continually start over. As compassionate leaders, we want to encourage people to do that. What do I need to hold on to? What do I need to let go of? What do I need to learn? Those are truly questions of power.

The Leader as "Merchant Priest"

When we approach the notion of business having a soul to journey toward (and with), by definition, we position the running of a business as a spiritual discipline. As we mentioned previously, when we introduced the use of the word priest, it in no way has any religious connotation. We mean spiritual in a way that is aligned with Aristotelian philosophy as well as the teachings of philosophers, sages, and mystics throughout the ages. It is the recognition that our sciences are concluding that consciousness proceeds matter, and that all matter is imbued with an unknowable life force that is the animating or vital force inherent in all living things. And, that that life force is a unity that is common to all.

The compassionate leader in this model aspires to a higher state of consciousness. They are exemplars of a possibility. One of the main axioms of leadership is that people will give me what they perceive I'm willing to accept. They will never give me what I ask for. That perception is often unconscious and is seldom recognized at an objective level. Most people pride themselves on being reasonable. And reasonable people will tend to get reasonable results. Make no mistake, people who urge you to be reasonable generally want you to accept their version of reality. Leaders are always in the process of creating the ceiling that people can rise to. Hopefully, it will be an unreasonable ceiling indeed!

One of the things that we do as leaders is to design the future through our expectations and conduct. We establish a metaphoric ceiling of what's possible. We do this through our consciousness. We do it through the ways that we view the world. We do it through articulating possibilities that we envision. We do this by creating a "reality distortion field" that captures people's imaginations, yearning, and aspirations. Then we organize conversations and we coordinate behaviors. We mediate our inner "resonance" with the intent of impacting external "resonance".

Consider Steve Jobs' infamous "reality distortion field". This is a term coined by Bud Tribble at Apple Computer, to describe Jobs' charisma and its effects on the developers working on the Macintosh project. Tribble said that the term came from an episode ("The Menagerie") in the television series *Star Trek*. In the episode, the reality distortion field was used to describe how aliens created their own new world through mental force. The reality distortion field was said by long-time Apple programmer Andy Hertzfeld to be Steve Jobs' ability to convince himself and others to believe almost anything with a mix of charm, charisma, bravado, hyperbole, marketing, appeasement, and persistence. The reality distortion field was said to distort a listener's sense of proportion and scales of difficulties and make them believe that the task at hand was possible. That is the process of leadership! The "magic" begins when the leader insists that others behave today as if this new reality actually existed today.

Was Steve Jobs a merchant priest? We believe he was. It is said that the only book on his iPad when he died was a copy of *The Autobiography of a Yogi* by Paramanhnsa Yogananda. He was reputed to read the book once every year and arranged to have a copy provided to every person who attended his memorial service. When recounting his experience of receiving the box that contained his copy, Mark Benioff, CEO of Salesforce.com said he thought, "This is going to be good. I knew that this was a decision he made, and whatever it was, it was the last thing he wanted us all to think about. I look at Steve as a very spiritual person. He had this incredible realization – that his intuition was his greatest gift and he needed to look at the world from the inside out."[42]

We organize interactions with that intention in mind —that the ideal is possible and that every exterior has an interior. The ideal is an external expression of an inner force. The way that we intervene and interact as a merchant priest leader is from that position of this heightened, compassionate awareness. We're engaging our clients and our consumers and our vendors with the ideal that we are all connected. We act from that premise as leaders, and we hold that to be a self-evident truth. We honor the fact that everything our businesses interact with and produce is an external expression of an unknowable life force that is common to all. Compassion requires that we honor that source as being intrinsically valuable. Then we just let the world unfold under that ceiling, knowing that it will have room to evolve to where that ceiling is. When we get close to the ceiling, we raise the ceiling of possibility again. This is the process of evolving and of growth. It's a spiritual process. To give this reality distortion field a more formal name, this is a process called "ontological design".

This is a high bar. It's establishes an ever higher expectation for being a higher self. And if we, as leaders, live "as if" it's possible to function in this manner, we'll create greater awareness, invite more compassion, have more efficient movement and better coordination, and be more authentic. These are the qualities the leader acting as a merchant priest invokes and invites. The promise is a richer, fuller, more harmonious life that is made possible in direct proportion to how much of the unknowable "inner" we make visible.

It's important to be pragmatic about this because it can sound a lot like magical thinking. In fact, it's profoundly pragmatic. Think of a tuning fork: It vibrates at a certain frequency and serves as a way to coherently organize music. As a leader you will tune an organization to a frequency around which all activities are coordinated. That's what leaders are. They are that tuning fork. They hold that vibration as part of their state of being. Everything is vibration. Everything around us is in a constant state of vibration. The paper you are reading these words on is not static. It is vibrating at a specific frequency. As is the ink that comprises each letter of each word. Matter—all matter—is simply a probability wave that collapsed in resonance to a certain frequency and is now manifested in particle form. The higher I'm vibrating; the more resonance I will create in the field to vibrate with me. The leader is an invitation to vibrate at a certain frequency. What we're suggesting is that the "merchant priest" provides those around them with an embodied invitation to vibrate at a higher level.

Blaine had the great opportunity to spend some time with Archbishop Desmond Tutu several years ago. Archbishop Tutu received the Nobel Peace Prize in 1984, the Albert Schweitzer Prize for Humanitarianism in 1986, the Sydney Peace Prize in 1999, the Gandhi Peace Prize in 2007, and the Presidential Medal of Freedom in 2009. Blaine recounts how he walked away from his meeting feeling uplifted and immensely proud to be alive at this time. It wasn't so much because of the content of their conversation. It had more to do with the experience of the frequency that Archbishop Tutu was holding that Blaine stepped into. The conversation could have been about making hot chocolate and he would have had the same experience! Vibrationally, he felt more human; he felt more alive and more possible.

This is the gift that an aware compassionate leader brings, the ability to operate at that higher level of vibration. We are metaphysical beings. We are metaphysicians as leaders. We cause things to vibrate at many frequency levels. The higher we can set these frequencies, the greater the likelihood that our organizations will also vibrate at those frequencies. We can't overstate the need to attend to this.

What Are the Implications?

Before he wrote *The Wealth of Nations*, Adam Smith penned *The Theory of Moral Sentiments*. In that book, he stressed that capitalism had to have a moral foundation to be sustainable. Otherwise, the rift between the rich and the poor would lead to "the highest degree of disorder." Business organizations are the most dominant influencers and arbiters of transformational change for society as a whole. The opportunity and responsibility for business is to bring the awareness of that impact to greater definition. The future of business (and for the planet) is for business to make the future its business. To not do so will result in an unspeakable outcome. To do so, is our journey, which compassionate capitalists and compassionate leaders from all walks of life will lead. And make no mistake, it will require great compassion and great courage to make it so.

This requires a shift in consciousness to make it happen. There can be no renewal of our relationship with nature without a renewal of humankind. We need to get reoriented to the long-forgotten fact that we are an interconnected component of a much larger biosphere. And, that the biosphere itself—indeed, everything—is a manifestation of a creative consciousness. This is an assertion that is being borne out in the field of quantum physics.

Theoretical physicist Max Planck was the originator of quantum theory, garnering him the Nobel Prize in Physics in 1918. Quantum theory turned our understanding of the subatomic world upside down and is today fundamentally changing how objective reality is both viewed and experienced. This is important to our exploration of compassionate capitalism as a spiritual discipline and to a leader being a merchant priest. It speaks to how consciousness conspires to produce what we view and experience as reality. For Planck, this realization was so profound that he said, "I regard consciousness as fundamental. I regard matter as derivative from consciousness. We cannot get behind consciousness. Everything that we talk about, everything that we regard as existing, postulates consciousness."[43]

In 1924, French physicist Louis de Broglie, who won the Nobel Prize for Physics in 1929, proposed a theory that asserted that there is no fundamental difference in the makeup and behavior of energy and matter. His theory stated that on the atomic and subatomic level, either may behave as being made of either particles or waves. This theory became known as the *principle of wave-particle duality*: Elementary particles of both energy and matter behave, depending on the conditions, like either particles or waves. This has been corroborated numerous times via the famous double-slit experiments which Wikipedia describes as being "...a demonstration that light and matter can display characteristics of both classically defined waves and particles; moreover, it displays the fundamentally probabilistic nature of quantum mechanical phenomena."[44] According to Wikipedia, "The same experiment can in theory be performed with *any* physical system: electrons, protons, atoms, molecules, viruses, bacteria, cats, humans, elephants, planets, etc. In practice it has been performed for light, electrons, buckminsterfullerene, and some atoms. [Although]...it is practically impossible to realize experiments that directly reveal the wave nature of any system bigger than a few atoms, in general, quantum mechanics considers *all matter* as possessing both particle and wave behaviors."[45]

Then, in 1927, Werner Heisenberg, winner of the Nobel Prize in Physics in 1932, proposed that precise, simultaneous measurement of two complementary values – such as the position and momentum of a subatomic particle – is impossible. Contrary to the principles of classical Newtonian physics, the more precisely one value (say position) is measured, the more inaccurate will be the measurement of the other value (say momentum). This theory became known as the Uncertainty Principle, and through collaboration with Niels Bohr (Nobel Prize for Physics in 1922), was expanded and evolved into what is known as the Copenhagen Interpretation of Quantum Mechanics. It is this interpretation which prompted Albert Einstein's famous comment, "God does not play dice with the universe." It suggested that there is no objective reality—only probabilities that manifest into measurable phenomenon when an observer interferes with the wave function.

According to R.C. Henry, Professor of Physics and Astronomy at John Hopkins University, "A fundamental conclusion of the new physics also acknowledges that the observer creates the reality. As observers, we are personally involved with the creation of our own reality. Physicists are being forced to admit that the universe is a 'mental' construction."[46]

Pioneering English physicist, astronomer and mathematician Sir James Jeans, who received the Gold Medal of the Royal Astronomical Society in 1922, wrote, "The stream of knowledge is heading toward a non-mechanical reality; the universe begins to look more like a great thought than like a great machine. Mind no longer appears to be an accidental intruder into the realm of matter, we ought rather to hail it as the creator and governor of the realm of matter. Get over it, and accept the inarguable conclusion. The universe is immaterial – mental and spiritual."[47]

No lesser luminaries than Nikola Tesla and Albert Einstein amplify this when they say that, "If you want to find the secrets of the universe, think in terms of energy, frequency and vibration (Tesla)," and "What we have called matter is energy, whose vibration has been so lowered as to be perceptible to the senses. There is no matter (Einstein)." Lest we think that all of this is purely conjecture in the domain of science and philosophy, the Dalai Lama has this to say about the nature of reality: "Broadly speaking, although there are some differences, I think Buddhist philosophy and Quantum Mechanics can shake hands on their view of the world."[48]

The import of all this relative to our exploration of compassionate capitalism is that it already exists as a possibility—and our task as leaders is to cause movement that brings the possibility closer to a realizable probability. The challenge for those leaders who opt to serve as merchant priests is to hold a higher level of consciousness and to entrain those in their spheres of influence to do the same as well. Aggregated, the effect will be to collapse the wave function of probability so that the particles of a new reality are manifested. A reality informed and guided by compassion. A reality that honors the connectivity of all life. A reality designed to uplift the qualitative experience of existing on this planet for all who exist on this planet. At the end of our time here the earth, the planet will be fine. The world doesn't need to be saved. It does however need our compassion if we as a species are to have the home we aspire to.

Returning to the definition of "soul", it's worth recalling that it is defined in Aristotelian philosophy as the animating or vital force inherent in all living things. We use soul as a symbol for something that represents an innate, intrinsic life force. We prefer to call this force consciousness. Others may refer to God, Buddha, Krishna, Shiva, Allah, Spirit, or any other deity. As a species we are (as far as we know) the only one on the planet to use symbols such as these to represent our view of reality. In this sense, we hold that every exterior symbol is the manifestation of an interior force that gives it form. The words on this paper are symbols. They have meaning to you the reader, yet they are not the meaning itself. The ability to translate symbols into what gives rise to them is how we approach the "truth" of what is. The root of all of the errors humans have made over millennia can be traced to the inability to do this. By not recognizing that the symbol is imbued with a life force that gives it form keeps us from experiencing the truth that all is sourced from the same fount. Adam Smith rightly perceived the

Invisible Hand as an aspect of that ineffable interior in his economic model. Recognizing, honoring, and illuminating its presence is the job of the merchant priest. The exterior represented by the symbol of Compassionate Capitalism is imbued from the interior with a universal life force—a consciousness—that is connected to all.

To paraphrase English philosopher Thomas Troward, it is the unfortunate fate of the lazy of mind to be content with the exterior of anything. We can no longer afford to continue to be captured by our perceptions of external reality or held hostage to a learned human condition that keeps us separate from the rest of life. Recognizing that form is the result of expansion from a universal center is the principle that the mystery of life is built upon, and is the key to seeing the interior of every exterior. Life becomes richer, fuller, and more harmonious in proportion to how much of the inner life force we can make visible to ourselves and others.

Nature is a great teacher. It is a symbol in the broadest sense, and all that is in and of it is a symbol of that which constitutes its inner beingness. The inability to recognize the inner of every exterior is at the root of the poverty of meaning experienced by many today. Compassion is a way to bring visibility to the inner and, in doing so, it is a way to answer John Maynard Keynes' question of how we are to use our "freedom from pressing economic cares . . . to live wisely and agreeably and well."

The Golden Rule is present in all major religions. It is the admonition to honor the soul. It must be present in business and it's one of the places (politics being the other) it is likely to be missing. There is not an asterisk next to the Golden Rule saying "Does Not Apply in Business Situations." Our journey to the soul of business—and it does have one—is a courageous journey graced by compassion, emboldened by desire, and celebrated by life.

Tom Robbins wrote in *Fierce Invalids Home From Hot Climates*, "...the sea was the shade of blue that black could have been if it hadn't stepped over the line." Today, we are at serious risk of stepping over the line. This book is an invitation and a challenge to move us to being the best we can be. Blaine and David believe *Compassionate Capitalism* represents a compelling and pragmatic way for businesses and individual leaders to make a difference and keep us all on the right side of the line. You as a reader have an opportunity right here and now to take action that is generative and that puts us in a position to effect major change. What you do is important and the positive results you initiate will be significant. We encourage you to share these ideas and begin conversations that you perhaps have never had. Experiment, be willing to explore and test what you think are boundaries. Develop relationships that are based on compassion and be willing to ask for support. We're confident that you and your organizations will be the vanguards for our future.

TAKE ACTION NOW!

Blaine and David are in high demand as keynote speakers, and both are committed to bringing the ideas presented in this book to fruition. As a consultant and executive coach, Blaine works with leaders and organizations around the world to assist them in becoming compassionate companies. Through his role as Dean of Education, the World Business Academy is continuously adding to a rich curriculum of trainings and resources organized around the tenets of *Compassionate Capitalism* that your organization can access and utilize.

David's work with MeltzerMission.com is also aligned with these critical business issues. You can access his amazingly transformative Meltzer Mission Gratitude App in the Apple AppStore or through Google Play.

We would love to explore with you and your team ways in which you can implement the ideas we present in this book. You can obtain a *Compassionate Capitalism Quotient (CCQ)* assessment and a companion *Compassionate Capitalism Action Plan (CCAP)* from us at www.Compassionate-Capitalism.org. The CCQ serves as a starting point for assessing your organization's *Compassionate Capitalism Quotient*. The CCAP provides suggestions and guidelines for putting in place simple and immediate steps you and your company can take to leverage the power of compassion in your daily activities. You can also explore a very informative FAQ section on the website.

Finally, you can reach out to either Blaine or David directly for inquires about interviews, speaking engagements, media appearances, or speaking to you and/or your executive team about *Compassionate Capitalism*. We can be contacted directly at the websites listed below or you can use the "**contact**" link at www.Compassionate-Capitalism.org. A member of one our teams will respond to your inquiry as soon as possible.

Blaine Bartlett can be contacted at www.blainebartlett.com.
David Meltzer can be contacted at www.meltzermission.com.

ACKNOWLEDGEMENTS

As with all undertakings of any significance, this book is not solely the work of the authors. There are professionals that assisted in guiding the creative process, and there are friends and family that provided the emotional and spiritual sustenance necessary to keep things on track. It's important that they and their contributions be acknowledged and witnessed.

From Blaine: I want foremost to acknowledge my wife Cynthia Kersey for her support, encouragement, solicited and unsolicited feedback, and good humored tolerance as I disappeared for hours on end to put word to paper; Rob Kosberg and his team at Best Seller Publishing for their expertise and flexibility; Cliff Carle for his incredible editing acumen and the numerous suggestions that helped make this book much more readable; Peggy McColl for her encouragement and willingness to consider the possibility of this topic for a book; Doug Rauch for sharing his story about Daily Table; David Meltzer who, as my co-author, brought a mind to bounce up against that helped shape the ideas in this book and make them practical. And to those upon whose shoulders I stood when beginning to think of how the world of business could be different and that are championing an awakened consciousness of what it means to be connected to all. Thank you to all!

From David: to my beautiful wife Julie and my M & M's Marissa, Mia, Marlena and Miles as well as anyone else that feels they should be acknowledged...and my mom!

Endnotes

1   Daniel Pinker, *The Better Angels of Our Nature: Why Violence Has Declined*, Penguin Books, 2012.

2   John Maynard Keynes, *The General Theory of Employment, Interest, and Money*, Harcourt, Brace & World, 1965.

3   Ayn Rand, Nathaniel Branden, Alan Greenspan, and Robert Hessen, *Capitalism: The Unknown Ideal*, New American Library, 1966.

4   See http://www.forbes.com/billionaires/list/.

5   See http://www.globalissues.org/article/26/poverty-facts-and-stats.

6   Pinker, *The Better Angels of Our Nature*.

7   Pinker, *The Better Angels of Our Nature*.

8   http://givingpledge.org/faq.aspx

9   http://www.overshootday.org

10 "Sen's Capability Approach," Internet Encyclopedia of Philosophy, http://www.iep.utm.edu/sen-cap/.

11 http://www.cdc.gov/nchs/products/databriefs/db241.htm

12 https://en.wikipedia.org/wiki/Market_system

13 https://en.wikipedia.org/wiki/Ideology

14 Fiona Macdonald, "NASA's Given Researchers $200,000 to Turn Human Poop into Food," http://www.sciencealert.com/nasa-s-received-a-200-000-grant-to-turn-human-poop-into-food.

15 http://www.theguardian.com/books/2015/jul/17/postcapitalism-end-of-capitalism-begun

16 http://www.firmsofendearment.com

17   http://www.npr.org/2014/07/28/335288388/when-did-companies-become-people-excavating-the-legal-evolution

18   Estimated hedge fund lobbying budget: nearly $40 million during the 2012 election cycle — more than double their contributions during the 2008 election cycle, according to opensecrets.org

19   Cecchetti and Scheonholtz, *Money, Banking, and Financial Markets (3rd ed.)*, (2005, pp. 225-6)

20   http://www.cgap.org/blog/10-myths-about-m-pesa-2014-update

21   http://www.cgap.org/blog/10-myths-about-m-pesa-2014-update

22   http://www.marketwatch.com/story/this-is-how-much-money-exists-in-the-entire-world-in-one-chart-2015-12-18

23   John Maynard Keynes, *Essays in Persuasion*, Macmillan, 1931, 198.

24   "Washing Hands Can Save 400 Children Everyday," http://www.khaleejtimes.com/lifestyle/health-fitness/washing-hands-can-save-400-children-everyday.

25   https://en.wikipedia.org/wiki/Leigh_Steinberg

26   http://www.theguardian.com/environment/2014/mar/03/tim-cook-climate-change-sceptics-ditch-apple-shares

27   Charles Darwin, *On the Origin of Species by Natural Selection*, London, 1859. "Survival of the fittest" was coined by Herbert Spencer in *Principles of Biology* (1964) as he drew parallels between his economic theories and Darwin's biological theories.

28   http://unstoppablefoundation.org

29   See http://w2.vatican.va/content/francesco/en/encyclicals/documents/papa-francesco_20150524_enciclica-laudato-si.html.

30   http://www.triplepundit.com/special/disrupting-short-termism/unilevers-handwashing-campaign-goes-beyond-csr-and-saves-lives/

31   http://worldbusiness.org

32   http://worldbusiness.org/fellows/

33   http://www.adweek.com/news/advertising-branding/ad-day-patagonia-136745

34   http://www.bloomberg.com/news/articles/2015-11-04/the-no-1-business-rule-of-this-billionaire-and-buddhist-priest

35   World Economic Forum, "The New Plastics Economy: Rethinking the Future of Plastics, 2016, http://www3.weforum.org/docs/WEF_The_New_Plastics_Economy.pdf.

36   Stephen Lewis, *Race against Time: Searching for Hope in AIDS-Ravaged Africa*, House of Anansi Press, 2006, 6.

37   https://en.wikipedia.org/wiki/Gaia_hypothesis

38   Schumann resonances are a set of spectrum peaks in Earth's electromagnetic field spectrum. https://en.wikipedia.org/wiki/Schumann_resonances

39   https://en.wikipedia.org/wiki/Microbiota

40   *Mehrabian, Albert (2009). "'Silent Messages' – A Wealth of Information About Nonverbal Communication (Body Language)". Personality & Emotion Tests & Software: Psychological Books & Articles of Popular Interest. Los Angeles, CA: self-published*. Retrieved April 6, 2010.

41   http://dailytable.org/about-us/our-story/

42   http://www.inc.com/hitendra-wadhwa/steve-jobs-self-realization-yogananda.html

43   https://en.wikiquote.org/wiki/Max_Planck

44   https://en.wikipedia.org/wiki/Double-slit_experiment

45   https://en.wikipedia.org/wiki/Copenhagen_interpretation

46   https://www.collective-evolution.com/2016/03/01/harvard-goes-to-the-himalayas-monks-with-superhuman-abilities-show-scientists-what-we-can-all-do/

47   https://books.google.ca/books?id=b-Ql0vz-ZmkC&printsec=frontcover#v=onepage&q&f=false

48   http://www.dalailama.com/news/post/905-quantum-physics---his-holiness-the-dalai-lama-participates-in-the-26th-mind--life-meeting-at-drepung---day-2

Made in the USA
Middletown, DE
02 March 2017